ROMANTIC
ENGLISH HOMES

ROMANTIC
ENGLISH HOMES

ROBERT O'BYRNE

photography by **Simon Brown**

CICO BOOKS

LONDON NEW YORK

Published in 2011 by CICO Books
An imprint of

Ryland Peters & Small
20–21 Jockey's Fields
London WC1R 4BW

519 Broadway, 5th Floor
New York, NY 10012

www.cicobooks.com

10 9 8 7 6 5 4 3 2

A CIP catalog record for this book is available
from the Library of Congress and the
British Library.

ISBN: 978 1 907563 29 4

Printed in China

Editor: Gillian Haslam
Designer: Paul Tilby
Photographer: Simon Brown

CONTENTS

OPPOSITE: Ornaments and bibelots
fill a corner of this late eighteenth-
century East End London house.

BELOW: Hand-printed paper covers
the walls of a Northumberland
farmhouse bedroom.

BOTTOM: Late nineteenth-century
damask, the colour of raspberry fool,
on the walls of Port Eliot, Cornwall.

INTRODUCTION

'The room had its bright, durable, sociable air, the air that Laura liked in so many English things,' wrote Henry James in his 1887 novella *A London Life*, before mentioning well-worn carpets, crisp chintz, bright wallpaper and 'fresh flowers wherever flowers could be put,' the whole ensemble giving the impression of 'being meant for daily life, for long periods, for uses of high decency.' Here James provides an admirable account of English domestic style, his assessment informed by an outsider's sympathetic awareness. Yet by the time *A London Life* was published, the English home had already reached its apogee and for all the appearance of resolute durability was under threat from the consequence of rising taxes and falling incomes. Like his fellow American Edith Wharton in her fiction, James was aware the object of his affection was vulnerable to change.

Even during the novelist's own lifetime a number of organisations came into existence intended to ensure the finest examples of English domestic design and decoration would survive for future generations' appreciation. The National Trust, for example, was founded in 1895, its stated purpose being the preservation for the benefit of the nation of land and buildings of importance. The majority of properties in the trust's care contain collections of pictures, furniture, books, metalwork, ceramics and textiles that might otherwise not have remained in their original settings. Left in context, they allow us to appreciate the nature of English taste, not least an addiction to collecting. Ever since the first English milord embarked on his Grand Tour in the seventeenth century, creating collections has been a national trait. By the time Henry James moved to England, the country's aristocratic palaces had become repositories of treasures from around the world. So too, albeit on a smaller scale, had almost every residence in England not least thanks to the spread of a global Empire. The Victorian home was frenziedly cluttered, holding a host of tables and display cabinets, sofas and armchairs, every surface covered with bibelots and gewgaws. Napoleon is believed to have observed the English are a nation of shopkeepers (in fact, the idea was first

TOP: **A set of pretty antique dessert plates help to conceal a jib door in Wembury, Devon.**

ABOVE: **An array of oriental ware lines the surface of a chest in High Hall, Suffolk.**

OPPOSITE: **Built in the sixteenth century, the hall in Mapperton, Dorset features a Jacobean overmantel installed in 1908 and an ornamented ceiling two decades later.**

proposed by Scottish economist Adam Smith in 1776) but this is only because they are also passionate consumers. If an Englishman's home is his castle, it is a meticulously decorated one. Since the nineteenth century the impression of massed objects has become a feature of the English interior, together with the intentional mixing of styles. In houses like Barrow Farm or Euridge Manor, classical will be placed next to gothic, tartan pattern mingled with floral print, one clashing colour lain beside the other. There is a kind of defiance in this eclecticism, evidence of an English self-belief that challenges the observer to question the outcome's authority.

Disparate accumulation leads to the notion all these pieces have been gathered over a long time and thanks to successive generations. Sometimes, as is the case with Port Eliot or Mapperton, this has been the case but in many instances the notion is illusory. Contrary to appearances, the collections at Restoration House and Greyhounds are recent, the result of diligent attendance at auction house and antique fair; such too was the case with the country house at the centre of one of Henry James' finest novels, *The Spoils of Poynton*. In this respect the English domestic interior can be perceived as a stage set on which the occupants perform roles of their choice.

At least part of the explanation for the widespread interest in the interior as a sort of historical pageant lies in the history of England herself, a country which – despite the best efforts of its neighbours – has never been invaded since 1066 and experienced little civil disruption for the past 350 years. It is a nation unaccustomed to social upheaval, a place where change comes slowly and meets a reluctant welcome. This is one of the reasons why England's historic houses act as backdrop for a host of popular novels like Evelyn Waugh's *Brideshead Revisited* or Daphne du Maurier's *Rebecca*, as well as many murder mysteries from Agatha Christie onwards. In films like Robert Altman's 2001 *Gosford Park* or the recent television series *Downton Abbey*, the eponymous house not only provides a setting but somehow transmogrifies into a key character. It is both the supposed timelessness of these properties and their many-layered appearance that makes them so alluring in fiction and fact alike. As susceptible as the rest of us to the depredations of time, thanks to the impression of an ancient past they propose their future immutability.

FAMILY HOUSES

DESPITE A RECENT, BUT BRIEF, FAD FOR MINIMALISM, THE TYPICAL ENGLISH INTERIOR REMAINS DISTINGUISHED BY ITS BUSYNESS. THIS IS TRUE EVEN OF SMALLER HOUSES WHERE IT MIGHT BE THOUGHT THERE WAS NO ROOM FOR MANY POSSESSIONS: IT IS A FEATURE OF THE ENGLISH CHARACTER TO DETECT EVERY AVAILABLE SURFACE AND THEN COVER IT WITH A VARIETY OF OBJECTS. JUST AS IMPORTANT AS THE NUMBER OF SUCH ITEMS IS THEIR DISPARITY. THE LESS THE PIECES MATCH ONE ANOTHER, THE MORE SUCCESSFUL THE RESULTING ENSEMBLE. BY THIS MEANS, THE IMPRESSION IS CONVEYED OF GENERATIONS OF THE SAME FAMILY HAVING INHABITED A HOUSE, EVEN IF IT HAS ONLY RECENTLY BEEN ACQUIRED.

OPPOSITE: When Greyhounds was gentrified into a private residence by Mrs Percival in 1906, she turned the former coaching inn's carriageway leading from Sheep Street to the rear terrace into a glazed hallway, a series of doors and windows providing protection from the elements.

ABOVE LEFT: Ten years ago Greyhounds acquired a new first-floor room, albeit incorporating much material salvaged from old buildings, which today serves as a library.

ABOVE CENTRE: Immediately behind the house is a slim parcel of land known as a burgage plot, derived from the Middle Ages when such narrow strips to the rear of each house were used as a garden or alternatively as additional space for outbuildings like workshops and stables. Freed from medieval constraints, further back it expands into the main garden and orchard.

ABOVE RIGHT: The house's present owners are both keen gardeners and have undertaken as much work outside as in. The glazed hallway is not only full of garden implements but also plants, doubling during the winter months as a greenhouse where bulbs are raised and delicate ferns given shelter from the cold.

GREYHOUNDS
OXFORDSHIRE

The south-west region of England known as the Cotswolds extends to almost 800 square miles, runs through several counties, and has no clearly defined borders. However, it is distinguished by both a landscape of gently rolling hillsides (the 'wolds') and an alluring honey-hued local limestone used for the majority of its buildings. In the later Middle Ages, especially the thirteenth to fifteenth centuries, the Cotswolds grew rich on the back of its sheep, the wool of which was highly prized throughout Europe; across the area there are substantial 'wool churches' erected during this period as a result of local residents' wealth.

One of the prettiest such churches, dedicated to St. John the Baptist, can be found in Burford, whose High Street rises steeply above a triple-arched medieval bridge over the river Windrush. There has long been a settlement here; at the time of the Domesday Book in 1087, Burford had a population of 200. It must have climbed rapidly thereafter because, by 1107, this was the first Cotswold town to be granted a market charter. Halfway up High Street and dating from around 1500 stands a half-timbered structure raised on stone pillars – the Tolsey where wool merchants once gathered and paid the local corporation's tolls or taxes.

Immediately beside it is Sheep Street, another indication of the importance of this trade to the town. Today the street is lined with a mixture of timbered and

In keeping with the early twentieth-century Arts and Crafts Movement's philosophy, the house's principal staircase was made from recycled older timbers.

stone-fronted houses, one of the latter today bearing the name Greyhounds. The history of this building parallels the fortunes of Burford, its origins as a wool merchant's house date from the late fifteenth century when the town was at its most prosperous. But land enclosures of the seventeenth and eighteenth centuries saw a sharp fall in demand for costly Cotswold wool and accordingly a decline in the entire area's wealth. By 1805, when the present stone frontage was added, Greyhounds had become a coaching inn and in the closing decades of the nineteenth century it was Thomas Paintin's Lenthall Temperance Hotel.

At the time, much of Burford had fallen into a sorry condition, its prosperity long forgotten and the charm of its architecture awaiting rediscovery. This only began around 1876 when the designer William Morris, visiting from his home at nearby

ABOVE LEFT AND RIGHT: The main staircase has been stripped of wax and limed with distemper. At its foot, the former dining room of the nineteenth-century temperance hotel has been turned into a sitting room, its walls distempered and the woodwork bleached to provide a gentle backdrop for English and Irish antique furniture.

ABOVE: A collection of china sits on an eighteenth-century mahogany occasional table before one of the sitting room's tapestries.

The sitting room is dominated by large verdure tapestries flanking an Irish c.1740 chimneypiece. Late eighteenth-century toile chintz covers the Irish side chairs and a 1930s chinoiserie table is flanked by 1953 coronation chairs.

OPPOSITE: Previously the library for the editor of *The Countryman* magazine, the kitchen with its mullioned recess overlooks the courtyard where, 150 years ago, Mr Paintin's horses were stabled. The ceiling beams came from a demolished Oxford pub and the mahogany chairs around the table are eighteenth-century Irish Gothick from County Limerick.

RIGHT: Only constructed in recent years, the garden pavilion at the very top of the orchard offers superlative views over the Windrush valley. All the interior fittings were salvaged from eighteenth-century Dublin tenement buildings and the painted floorboards are reused scaffolding planks. The walls are hung with Irish bird and flower pictures by Samuel Dixon (fl. 1748–1769) and his followers.

Kelmscott Manor, found the vicar of St. John the Baptist's scraping medieval wall-paintings from its interior. In the face of protests, the vicar is said to have responded, 'This church, sir, is mine, and if I choose to, I shall stand on my head in it.' The following year Morris helped to found the Society for the Preservation of Ancient Buildings (popularly known as the Anti-Scrape).

Later Burford vicars were more historically-minded, not least the Rev. William C. Emeris who in 1906 bought and restored a timbered house on Sheep Street. Two years later his sister, Elizabeth Percival, acquired neighbouring Greyhounds for £700 and not only undertook necessary work on the house but also greatly extended the plot of land that rises behind so that it now took in a small cottage originally occupied by a gardener; in the early 1930s this was rented by the Bloomsbury painters Duncan Grant and Vanessa Bell when Burford experienced a resurgence of popularity among artists and designers, with many older buildings undergoing considerate restoration. Close to the house, Mrs Percival also created a series of stone-flagged terraces with low retaining walls where horses had once been stabled. Greyhounds then passed

through a succession of equally sympathetic hands until 1946 when it became the publishing home of *The Countryman* magazine, founded twenty years earlier by J.W. Robertson Scott.

And so it remained for over half a century until bought in 1999 by Burford resident, antique dealer Michael Taubenheim and his partner, Irish paint specialist Christopher Moore. Since coming into their care, Greyhounds has undergone a transformation in keeping with William Morris's philosophy, to ensure the preservation of as much of the building's history as possible and to enhance further its already considerable charms. With 27 rooms, the house always rambled but often not in a manner that was practicable or even coherent; when it passed into the present owners' hands, for example, there were no less than five staircases.

Of these, the principal one appears to date from the time of Mrs Percival and, in keeping with the era's Arts and Crafts Movement

The intention has been to fill the house with abundance of light thanks to scrubbed woodwork, painted floors and seagrass.

philosophy, was made from recycled timbers. But this led only to a handful of rooms at the front of the house with no direct link to the immediate rear, so Taubenheim and Moore sensibly filled in this first-floor vacuum with a capacious library. Like many houses of its period, Greyhounds has small, mullion-paned windows. Therefore, explains Moore, 'the aim has been to fill the house with as much light as possible, resulting in scrubbed woodwork, limed surfaces, painted floors, pale walls, and seagrass.' Meanwhile, while they share a passionate engagement with the past, the two

OPPOSITE AND THIS PAGE: Filling in a space between the front and rear of the house, the first-floor library was built in 2001 and fitted with salvaged timber, including glazed doors from Dublin. The bookshelves hold not just an assortment of blue-and-white china but also an extensive collection of architectural and gardening books, and a complete run of *The Countryman* magazine, published at Greyhounds for over 50 years.

The free-standing tub in the master bathroom is strategically placed so that anyone using it is offered a wonderful axial view all the way up the garden to the orchard. On the far wall above an antique mahogany chest of drawers hangs an early nineteenth-century gouache view of Naples with Vesuvius erupting in the background.

RIGHT: This guest bedroom has been simply fitted out with a pair of box beds covered in French linen. On the walls are displayed a number of sepia views of Dublin's Liffey valley by Jonathan Fisher dating from the 1790s.

BELOW: Another guest room tucked beneath the eaves to the rear of the house benefits from wall-to-wall mullion windows which not only provide abundant light but also offer a splendid view of the box-planted courtyard and beyond this the upper garden.

With 27 rooms, the house always rambled but not necessarily in a practicable or coherent manner.

men's different backgrounds have resulted in the house's interior being a contented fusion of English and Irish taste. The beams in the kitchen, for example, came from a demolished Oxford pub while the sitting room chimneypiece was rescued from a field in Ireland. Nowhere is this blending of two cultures more successfully achieved than in a garden house that stands at the top of the garden: despite looking like a long-sited and representative Cotswold building, not only is this of recent construction but all its architectural features like doors, windows and architraves were salvaged from Irish properties. Below this, an acre of sloping gardens runs like a series of additional rooms towards the house, each section differentiated by its own herbaceous borders in which many of the plants have an Irish pedigree. Just over a century after it was reawakened from a long slumber, Greyhounds now rejoices in the full bloom of its beauty.

CLAVEY'S FARM
SOMERSET

In the Domesday Book completed in 1086, the Somerset village of Mells was known as 'Mulne' meaning several mills, thereby indicating the region's principal activity. However, by 1500 it was called Iron Burgh as a result of the iron ore extracted in the area. No trace is visible in the village of such activities, nor indeed of the coal mines which operated in this part of the country during the eighteenth and nineteenth centuries. Instead, like much of the surrounding region, Mells, which is dominated by the imposing spire of fifteenth-century St. Andrew's Church, has now become principally known for its quietly picturesque charm.

That charm is due to no small extent to improvements carried out by the Horner family which acquired the Mells estate around the time of the Dissolution of the Monasteries in 1539 and nurtured their property over the succeeding centuries. In the Victorian era the notion began to spread that the popular nursery rhyme about Little Jack Horner actually referred to Thomas Horner, steward to the last abbot of Glastonbury. According to this story,

OPPOSITE: Dating from around the close of Elizabeth I's reign, Clavey's Farm is built of undressed local limestone which is still quarried not far from the house. Because this is so hard to cut, the window surrounds and door hood were carved from the area's softer stone, Doulting, its tractability also seen in Glastonbury Abbey and the west facade of Wells Cathedral.

ABOVE RIGHT: Clavey's Farm has some two acres of gardens, including a paddock. An ardent gardener, before she started the present planting Fleur Kelly cleared away ground elder and other invasive weeds by allowing pigs to graze on the land.

RIGHT: Stone walls, steps and pathways enclose the farm's garden that features fulsome borders replete with flowering shrubs and perennials like roses and delphiniums.

LEFT AND ABOVE: Opening directly off the garden, the former estate manager's office now serves as the Kellys' drawing room. The substantial stained pine bookcase came from Dundee Library in Scotland: it was one of several rescued from a skip by a friend of the family.

OPPOSITE: The tongue-and-groove dado panelling and the chimneypiece are nineteenth century and date from the room's time as an estate manager's office. The door to the right opens into a walk-in safe, used to hold money received from the estate's tenants.

prior to the monastery's destruction Horner was sent by the Abbot to Henry VIII in London with a large Christmas pie containing deeds to a dozen manors owned by Glastonbury. However, before reaching his destination, he put his hand inside the dish and extracted the deeds of the Mells estate, keeping these for himself. The veracity of the tale was consistently denied by later members of the family, the last male relative of which, Edward Horner, died during the First World War; he is commemorated inside St. Andrew's Church by a superb bronze equestrian statue by Sir Alfred Munnings on a base designed by Sir

Edwin Lutyens. The Mells estate subsequently passed to his sister, Katherine, who had married Raymond Asquith, son of Prime Minister H.H. Asquith. Her husband, like her brother, was killed while on active service in France but the Asquith family remains in ownership of Mells.

Probably at some point in the nineteenth century, a property some half a mile outside the village came to serve as a residence for the Horner estate's agent. This is Clavey's Farm, a six-bedroom, stone-built house with tiled roof. The agent's office was added during this era, a handsome space half-panelled in tongue-and-groove

Examples of Fleur Kelly's historically-inspired painting can be seen in every room in the house.

boards and with a much higher ceiling than any other part of the house. The decor was clearly intended to impress tenants coming to pay their rent: a door off the room opens into a walk-in safe where money received on these occasions would have been stored. Elsewhere in the building, other interior changes seem to have been made around the same time, such as the introduction of parquet flooring, panelled doors and a cornice in the entrance hall.

Externally, although owing much of its present appearance to an overhaul in the early eighteenth century, the main part of the building is believed to have been constructed around 1600 just as the reign of Henry VIII's daughter, Elizabeth I, was drawing to a close. The front retains mullion windows of the period but also has a later, beautifully curved hood above the front door, typical of those found in similar properties throughout the region. As for its name, supposedly this derives from an

ABOVE LEFT: Inside the main part of the house, an open door offers a view from the entrance hall to the sitting room. When the building provided a residence for the Mells estate manager, it was gentrified with the addition of such decorative elements as the cornicing and parquet flooring.

ABOVE: In a corner of the sitting room hangs one of Fleur Kelly's paintings of an angel, inspired by an extant fresco in the French Romanesque Abbey Church of Saint-Savin-sur-Gartempe.

OPPOSITE: The sitting room is located in the oldest part of the house and the small glazed cupboard to the left of the chimneypiece was once part of a larger hearth. The neo-classical gilt overmantle came from Francis Kelly's father who had stored it in a barn.

earlier occupant, a Mr Clavey who kept horses here to service the mailcoach service running between Bath and London, even though Mells is somewhat off the main route between these two cities.

Whatever its origins and previous mixed usage, for the past decade the farm has been home to Francis and Fleur Kelly, he a historic buildings expert, she an artist. Fleur Kelly specialises in fresco and panel painting, having trained in Prato, near Florence, with renowned painter, conservator and teacher Leonetto Tintori. While often commissioned to create new murals or restore

Visitors to the house are likely to consider its limewashed interiors charmingly unspoilt and chock-full of artworks and curiosities.

old ones, when living at Clavey's Farm she operates from a studio within the house and in her panel painting, examples of which can be seen in almost every room, works in gesso, a traditional technique involving a binding agent mixed with chalk, gypsum and pigment and then carefully built up in layers. Given her training, it is not surprising that Fleur's pictures are usually inspired by art history, with regular references being found in them to paintings from the medieval and Renaissance periods. This engagement with art history must be something of a family trait, since in the kitchen

OPPOSITE: The farm's kitchen is original to the house and includes an impressive fireplace made of Doulting stone. While the doors and window shutters are original, sadly the old floor flagstones were taken up at some date in the last century as part of an earlier occupant's programme of 'modernisation' that the present owners have done their best to reverse.

ABOVE AND LEFT: The kitchen table was discovered, encrusted with grease and scarred by nail marks, in a garage in Bath; none of the benches and seats around it match one another.

hangs a still-life painting by Fleur's father-in-law, Peter Kelly, inspired by the work of the post-Impressionists. Most of the house's furnishings, some of them inherited, others bought, are equally imbued with the patina of history. And thanks to boldly inventive use of colour on the limewashed walls, the house looks as though it has been occupied by almost as many generations of Kellys as there were of Horners.

Yet according to Fleur, when the couple moved into Clavey's Farm at the start of the new millennium, the house bore abundant evidence of its most recent and unfortunate 'modernisation' undertaken in the 1960s: the couple have since done their best to remove most of this. Some of the previous residents' interventions could not be removed. In the kitchen, for example, the flagstone flooring had been taken out and replaced by cement. But wherever possible, the Kellys have restored and preserved, taking care to make sure old window shutters still work and fires can still burn in all the rooms. 'Local folklore reports that we've returned it to the Stone Age!' Fleur jests. Visitors to the house, on the other hand, are sure to consider it a perfect reflection of four centuries of Mells history.

ABOVE TOP LEFT AND RIGHT: In a corner of Francis Kelly's bedroom stands an old mahogany mirror, its glass heavily foxed but still able to reflect some of Fleur's paintings, including the large female nude inspired by a picture of Mary Magdalene produced by the fifteenth-century Flemish artist Rogier van der Weyden.

OPPOSITE: Francis Kelly's half-tester bed was bought at an auction in Bath. Fleur only later discovered there had been no other bidders for the item because it was too short: they had to add a section in order to make it serviceable. The old suitcase beneath the bed serves as a shoe box.

OPPOSITE: A pair of doors, their upper sections made from sash windows found on the street, leads into the basement kitchen with its scrubbed table bought by Tim Whittaker's father in Whitby, Yorkshire.

ABOVE LEFT: Whittaker inserted the corner cupboard using recycled timber. The upper section holds part of a copper batterie de cuisine and a well-polished late eighteenth-century copper tea urn.

ABOVE CENTRE: In the adjacent scullery most of the space is taken up by a range of drawers and shelving originally made for a pharmacy in Spitalfields, London; the sink came from a nearby derelict house.

ABOVE RIGHT: Much of the back of the house is taken up by a generous bay, which makes the most of the afternoon light coming across the formal garden, planted by Whittaker.

NEW ROAD
LONDON

Perhaps no other district of London has undergone so many highs and lows as the East End. In the Middle Ages, the area was monastic property and also used as a royal hunting ground. But when England's importance as a maritime state started to grow in the sixteenth century, so too did the magnitude of the port of London and of the Royal Navy's shipyards, both of which were located in this part of the capital. Related industries, like the manufacture of gun powder and rope-making, likewise flourished in the East End.

The Great Fire of London in September 1666 was followed by major rebuilding in the old city. Within two decades came new settlement to the immediate east as industrious French immigrants known as Huguenots sought refuge in London following the proscription of the Protestant faith in their native country. The Huguenots were noted for their weaving of fine silks and they were followed by further waves of economic refugees who likewise became engaged in various aspects of the clothing trade: impoverished Irish, Eastern European Jews, and, in the second half of the last century, Bangladeshis and Pakistanis. Yet while fabric and clothing production employed large numbers of local residents, so too did activities associated with London's expanding port, bringing produce to England from its colonies around the world. The West India Docks, where goods could be unloaded directly into quayside

warehouses, were established in 1803, construction on London Docks began in 1805, and on the East India Docks a year later. This led to a further demand for housing, such as the properties built in the final years of the eighteenth century by a developer called Barnes; on a site acquired from nearby London Hospital he gave his new thorough-fare the self-explanatory name of New Road. Since 2000, one of its larger properties has been home to Tim Whittaker who runs the Spitalfields Trust (a charity dedicated to restoring Georgian houses) and his partner, chef Harvey Cabaniss. The house's original residents are unknown, but by the 1840s it was occupied by a family with strong maritime connections, one being a sea captain, another a ship builder, and a third a ship chandler trading

Although the building had not been used as a private residence for the previous eighty years, Whittaker was undeterred.

from a shop in the basement. However, the family moved out the following decade as this part of London began to go into seemingly irreversible decline. Even by 1800 the East End had become known for its overcrowded houses, many of which deteriorated into slums, and for the related problems of poverty and crime. An abundance of semi-

OPPOSITE: This handsome early nineteenth-century mahogany bureau was bought by Whittaker on eBay. The chair in front dates from the 1730s and came from Cumbria, as did Whittaker's childhood teddy bears.

THIS PAGE: The house's old basement kitchen is now a snug sitting room, after Whittaker had lowered the floor level and removed the timber between beams. The mahogany drop-leaf table is late eighteenth century.

OPPOSITE: The biggest space on the ground floor is now given over to the main bedroom, with the bed, like so much else in the house, constructed from a variety of sources, its top being made of an old window pelmet.

ABOVE: The bedroom's lacquer grandfather clock dates from the 1760s while the oak closed stool (used to hold a chamber pot) is also eighteenth century; on it sits a late seventeenth-century prayer cushion.

RIGHT: Above an assembled chimneypiece in the front study hang two eighteenth-century engravings of Wentworth Woodhouse in Yorkshire and Burlington House in London. The black basalt urn dates from the 1760s.

and unskilled labour on the docks led to low wages and poor conditions, and anyone with aspirations to respectability headed west. Whittaker's house suffered from lack of care over the next 150-odd years, being occupied in succession by Scottish linen drapers, Jewish tailors and then Asian clothes manufacturers until ending as wholesale premises for market stallholders.

Although none of the building had been used as a private residence for the eighty years before his purchase, Whittaker was undeterred. Nor did he find the amount of work needed to turn the house back into a home disconcerting. In the basement, for example, the back room had a ceiling so low that it was almost impossible for

LEFT AND ABOVE: Directly beneath the study's two windows looking onto New Road sits a late nineteenth-century French zinc bath in which Whittaker lies and cogitates. The little mahogany Pembroke table to its left is late eighteenth century, the chair early nineteenth.

OPPOSITE: Through the study's door is a view of the entrance hall and beyond it of the office, the wall above its chimney dominated by a French nineteenth-century rococo-revival gilt frame.

anyone entering to stand upright. So he took up the old flagstones and dug down some seven inches before laying a concrete floor which was then covered with the original flags. Meanwhile, unable to raise the ceiling height, he removed the timber boards and left just the joists, thereby at least giving the impression of more space.

The ground floor required equally radical intervention, since all the room partitions had been taken out, probably sometime in the nineteenth century, to make one big space interrupted only by the stairs. Remnants of cornice work and marks on the timber floor – buried beneath

another covering – indicated where the original walls would have been and these were duly reinstated, with missing sections of cornicing replaced. The wall panelling and chair rails in the ground-floor rooms are testament to Whittaker's initiative since they were all assembled from a variety of salvaged material, as were many of the house's other furnishings. Both the painted chimneypiece in the bedroom, for example, and the early nineteenth-century mahogany bureau in the study were bought on eBay. Other items, especially those used for the construction of doors, fitted cupboards, and internal windows, were found in

Work continues on the house, most recently the refurbishment of what would have been the first-floor main reception room.

THIS PAGE AND OPPOSITE: When Whittaker first bought the house, the first-floor drawing room had become a sweatshop with a false ceiling. He has recently finished its restoration, putting back shutters, dado panelling, architraves and a late eighteenth-century fireplace originally from Rodney Street in Liverpool. Above the last of these hangs a Grand Tour portrait of a young gentleman by Richard Brompton, portrait painter to Catherine the Great of Russia, while the facing alcove holds a portrait of the wealthy Swiss-born merchant and banker Anthony Francis Haldimand by Jean-François Rigaud. The bed, recently made using old posts, is covered in mauve French toile of a scene by 'David', c. 1810.

skips or rescued from the street. Furniture has come from a wide variety of sources – in the downstairs sitting room is a papier-mâché wall clock bought by Whittaker's great, great, great-grandfather for his wife in the 1860s, while a library chair was bought in Rochester and brought back to London on the train.

Whittaker admits his approach to the house's refurbishment has not been conducted according to rigorous historic principles; in a number of instances he inserted internal windows so as to increase the amount of light throughout the house. The upper section of the little ground-floor office is glazed, allowing the hall to avoid near-darkness.

The most substantial addition to the property took place not long after its purchase: the construction of a summer house in the back garden. For a long time this was free-standing; only in 2007 was it connected to the house by a glazed link which doubles as conservatory. Meanwhile, the west-facing garden which benefits from afternoon light was laid out in a formal style with yew and box topiary. Work continues on the house, most recently the refurbishment of what would have been the main reception room on the first floor, a handsome space with three windows overlooking the street. More remains to be done on this and the floor above, no doubt taking place as Whittaker and Cabaniss continue their acquisitions of suitable salvage.

LEFT: The temple's south side is given over to an orangery in which delicate plants would be stored during winter, kept warm by a hypocaust around the perimeter. In summer, the sash windows were entirely removed, transforming this space into an open pavilion. The stuccodore responsible for the ceiling's elaborate neo-classical plasterwork is unknown.

ABOVE: Beneath a dome sheeted in lead, the red sandstone used to construct the temple was quarried within the estate and has survived remarkably well for almost 250 years. However, by the early 1980s the building was in need of major restoration, with rain coming into many of the rooms: since then it has been made watertight.

BELOW: The Temple contains two limestone spiral staircases, one of which runs 54 steps from basement to attic.

TEMPLE OF DIANA
STAFFORDSHIRE

The eighteenth-century historian Edward Gibbon who embarked on a tour of continental Europe in 1763 later remarked, 'According to the law of custom, and perhaps of reason, foreign travel completes the education of an English gentleman.' The Grand Tour, as it came to be known, originated in the seventeenth century and soon became an obligatory part of the upbringing of every Englishman who wished to be regarded as well-informed. Sometimes lasting several years, the voyage's culmination was a sojourn in Rome, not least for the opportunity this afforded to explore the city's classical ruins. The experience would influence generations of travellers' taste, particularly in the classical-style houses they commissioned as homes on their return to England.

But the Grand Tour also affected the appearance of the English landscape, thanks both to the impression made on foreign visitors by the Roman Campagna's pastoral beauty and to the landscape paintings they saw – and bought – by earlier artists like Nicolas Poussin and Claude Lorrain. Sometimes the inspiration can be easily traced. The park at Stourhead in Wiltshire, for example, designed by Henry Hoare II and laid out between 1741 and 1780 is known to have been inspired by Claude, Poussin and most particularly Gaspar Dughet. The irony is that it

LEFT TOP AND BOTTOM: A vaulted basement kitchen has been installed in what had originally been the dairy; one of the dairy slabs still survives. When the present occupant moved into the building, this room's walls were dark purple with damp, but sufficient heating now keeps them dry.

ABOVE AND OPPOSITE: The Temple was designed to include this Music Room with its delicate plasterwork believed to be by Joseph Bromfield. The 1817 Broadwood piano is still in working order, as can be testified by its owner who plays the instrument while sitting on a 1820s Biedermeier chair bought for £25 in a market.

should have been a group of predominantly French artists working in Italy who had such a powerful impact on the development of what became known as the 'English Garden' not least because this in turn became fashionable in France and Italy.

The key feature of the eighteenth-century English Garden was that unlike those created earlier it appeared to be entirely natural despite being a work of artifice. At least part of the naturalistic effect was achieved by the use of very few elements, predominantly grass, trees and water. The only overt evidence of man's

THIS PAGE AND OPPOSITE: **The former dairymaid's room on the ground floor is now a comfortable sitting room, not least thanks to the addition of a wood-burning stove two years ago. The oil above the chimneypiece is called 'The Rehearsal' and was painted by the twentieth-century classicist Victor Moody who spent much of his life as principal of Malvern School of Art. The neo-Gothic barrel organ was probably made by J. Hicks of Bristol, whose name is on each of the barrels, eight of which hold ten hymns apiece. Restored in the 1990s, it came from Langstone Court, Herefordshire.**

The various ground-floor rooms show the building was ingeniously designed by Paine to serve a number of different purposes.

intervention would be the siting of a temple or monument to close a vista. Among the most influential men working in this field was landscape designer Lancelot Brown, more commonly known as Capability Brown, responsible for some 200 such gardens across England where the results came to be known as 'Brownifications'. Two years after his death in 1783, he was described as the 'omnipotent magician' by William Cowper who in 'The Task' wrote 'He speaks, The lake in front becomes a lawn/Woods vanish,

hills subside, and valleys rise...' One of the patrons for whom Brown undertook such work was the politician Sir Henry Bridgeman. Originally from Devon, the Bridgeman family had risen in the world during the previous century thanks to the industry of Orlando Bridgeman, an ambitious lawyer created first baronet in 1660. Just over a century later his descendant Sir Henry, later Baron Bradford, inherited estates in Staffordshire from an uncle and employed Brown there to lay out a new park. The old

THIS PAGE AND OPPOSITE: **Ever**
since the Temple was constructed in
the early 1770s, this has been known
as the Tea Room. Its walls carry a
series of canvases and grisaille panels
relating the story of the Roman
goddess Diana; these were painted
in 1775 by the Swiss-born artist
Giovanni Battista Innocenzo Colombo.
Despite restoration, the pictures have
darkened over time and therefore no
longer encourage the impression of
interior merging with the surrounding
parkland as must have been the case
when they were first installed. The
white marble chimneypiece is a
nineteenth-century replacement
of the original.

house at its centre likewise underwent modification
thanks to the designs of Palladian architect James Paine.
He was also commissioned to produce the plans for a
'Roman' bridge and a temple constructed in Capability
Brown's park.

The latter structure must have been designed by
1768, the year in which stone was quarried for it
within the park. And building work was concluded by
1775 when Giovanni Battista Innocenzo Colombo was
paid for murals in the Temple's circular Tea Room. Born
in the Lugano region of Switzerland in 1717, Colombo
was from a family of decorative painters and came to

England in 1774, exhibiting landscapes at the Royal
Academy and designing scenery for the King's Theatre
in London.

Inside the Temple, he painted scenes depicting exploits
of the ancient Roman goddess Diana; these still retain
their contemporary written captions. The choice of
subject reflects the era's interest in classical mythology,
Diana being traditionally associated with wild animals
and woodland, and oak groves being held sacred to her.
The design of the Tea Room, with its curved walls and
shallow saucer dome, was intended to suggest a pavilion
with openings to Brown's classically-inspired landscape

THIS PAGE AND OPPOSITE: The Tea Room's colour scheme is not original and dates from the restoration of the 1990s. The chairs here are of the sort christened 'Yorkshire Drunkards' Chairs' by a Victorian antique dealer, a term which has ever since stuck. Two of them are Chinese Export of the 1760s made in huanghuali (otherwise known as Chinese Rosewood) and may have come to England in kit form. The other pair is English-made in mahogany. The design, found in large numbers in many houses, seems to derive from a long set of chairs of the 1740s from the Sub-Hall at Houghton in Norfolk. The square piano of 1792 was made by Longman and Broderip and remains in excellent condition; as with the instrument in the Music Room, it is regularly played. Both on the Regency dumb waiter and the dining table are some parts of a large 1840s Bloor Derby dinner service.

immediately outside, although since Colombo's paintings have darkened over the past two centuries the allusion is less apparent than would originally have been the case.

This is only one of a number of rooms on the ground floor of the building which was ingeniously designed by Paine to serve a number of different purposes, and displays two quite distinct facades. In addition to the Tea Room, the adjacent octagonal Music Room was also intended for use by the residents of the main house and their guests for whom a visit to the Temple would have involved a pleasant stroll across the park.

Both rooms are on the north side of the building, the exterior of which rises to a broken pediment interrupted by a domed projection, a favourite conceit of the architect. Meanwhile the opposite side of the building contains a large orangery in the form of a glazed loggia with balustrade concealing the pitched roof behind. Inside this space is elliptical in form, its high coved ceiling covered in neo-classical stucco work. Paine is supposed to have described this as 'my greenhouse.' If so it is certainly the most splendid greenhouse imaginable.

OPPOSITE AND ABOVE: The Temple's main bedroom is located above the Tea Room and beneath the dome (which houses the building's water tanks). The bed is an amalgam of pieces from the seventeenth and nineteenth centuries as well as more recent elements. Having been assembled inside the room in the 1990s, it is now a permanent fixture.

RIGHT: The guest bedroom, which the Temple's present occupant calls the Thin Room, sits above the sitting room and beneath one side of the north facade's pediment, hence its pitched roof. A recess under the wall beam allowed for a series of bookcases to be installed here.

Nor is this the end of the Temple's intended functions since its basement, which now contains a kitchen, was to be used 'as dairies and for other purposes appertaining thereto' while the ground floor held a room for 'the habitation of the dairy woman' and there was also 'an exceedingly good bedchamber' over the centre and another bedroom tucked into the top of the building.

In recent years the Temple has been converted into a private residence; during the 1990s it was home to Mr and Mrs Janney who contributed to the building's restoration. They were succeeded by its present occupant Jeffrey Haworth, an architect who worked first as Historic Buildings Representative and then Curator for the National Trust. Founder-Chairman of the Hereford and Worcester Gardens Trust and a well-known expert on English houses and families, he was retained by Simon Jenkins to advise on both accuracy of historical fact and opinions expressed in the latter's 2003 book *England's Thousand Best Houses*.

HIGH HALL
SUFFOLK

Alan Dodd has spent the greater part of his life painting murals, examples of which can be found in some of London's most beautiful buildings: a Pompeian ceiling based on unexecuted drawings at the Sir John Soane's Museum; the reinstated trompe l'oeil decoration on Vardy's balustrade for the great staircase of 1757 at Spencer House; and three large landscape canvases replacing lost work by Antonio Zucchi for the Great Eating Room at Home House in Portman Square.

OPPOSITE: Beneath the ground floor dining room's six-compartment ceiling stand a set of oak Montgolfier-backed chairs around a gate-legged table. The late nineteenth-century Louis XV-revival leaf-drop chandelier adds to the French provincial character of the room.

ABOVE LEFT AND RIGHT: The exterior of the seventeenth-century house at dusk. Thanks to the tall red brick chimney, the building was nicknamed Mustard Pot Hall by local children.

Dodd's own home, although not in London, is likewise a tribute to his exemplary skills. High Hall in Suffolk looks as distinctively idiosyncratic as one of its present owner's pictures. Of red brick softened by time and with a high-pitched roof covered in red tiles, the building's origin and purpose are uncertain. However, it appears to have been constructed during the first decades of the seventeenth century by Thomas Rede (born 1613), whose initials were placed on the west front and who lived nearby at Weston Hall.

The latter house had been erected by Thomas's grandfather, John Rede, MP for Guildford in 1547 and Sheriff of Surrey in 1575. Sadly only a fragment of Weston Hall now survives: following a fire in 1821, the greater part of the building was demolished. In Alfred Suckling's *History and Antiquities of the County of Suffolk* published in 1846, mention is made of High Hall, described as 'a small but curious edifice of red brick... The interior of this fanciful little dwelling is finished rather expensively with moulded cornices and wrought

ceilings; and though still two storeys high, was originally much loftier. It is said to have been erected for a summerhouse, as its upper floor commanded a view of the German Ocean, but tradition relates that it was early converted to a purpose far less innocent.'

Quite what Suckling imagined that purpose to have been must remain a matter of conjecture, and his notion that the building was 'much loftier' also has to be called into question since that would have further distorted its already unusually elevated contours. Most likely High Hall was always a pleasure house, without any need for hypothesizing what form that pleasure might have taken. Alan Dodd thinks the house originally was intended as a dower dwelling for Weston Hall, but whatever was the case, by the eighteenth century it had become a cottagers' residence and remained such until occupied by the agent of a local estate in the second half of the last century. As the quoins down every corner indicate, the house was always free-standing but around 1965 a wing was added at right angles.

Twenty years later, High Hall came to Dodd's attention when he was looking for a house in the area. That it survives to this day is purely thanks to his tenacity; just as he was about to complete the purchase, the house was gutted by fire. Such a setback might have deterred other prospective buyers but given that much of Dodd's

ABOVE LEFT AND RIGHT: In the kitchen a plethora of crockery on the oak-grain dresser includes a set of Mason's vase and table stone china and a number of caneware jugs. The framed painting of Glastonbury Tor is by Diana Howard.

OPPOSITE: Cases of Victorian stuffed birds flank the kitchen's double doors, their upper sections made using zinc-latticed windows from a now-demolished stable block believed to have been designed by James Wyatt.

RIGHT: The coral-coloured 'panelling' covering the walls of the first-floor drawing room is an example of Alan Dodd's trompe l'oeil skills. As with the room beneath, the ceiling is sectioned by plaster moulded beams, with the addition of a heavy ornamental cornice below. The large chair is Chinese blackened beech from around 1800.

> Most likely High Hall was always a pleasure house, without hypothesizing what form that pleasure took.

work involves acts of resuscitation, he was prepared to take on the challenge of restoring his new home.

Fortunately, while the interior was blackened by smoke and the staircase, another 1960s addition, effectively destroyed the building remained otherwise structurally sound. Nevertheless, Dodd's first major undertaking was to restore the seventeenth-century plasterwork ceilings to their original condition and to assimilate the 1960s wing so that it blended harmoniously with the main building. Having previously reflected the era in which it was added now he prefers to believe the wing looks as though dating from around the start of the nineteenth century. This transformation has been aided by sensitive supplements such as the zinc-latticed windows which came from a now-demolished stable block nearby believed to have been designed by James Wyatt. Today the wing accommodates a kitchen, two bedrooms and bathroom, the last of these featuring a chaise percée for the lavatory.

The older part of the building is accessed through the entrance corridor, the walls of which, despite the narrowness of space, have been covered with fragments of printed red linen in which the Tudor rose features prominently. From here, one enters High Hall's ground floor which today serves as a dining room. Heavy mouldings divide

its ceiling into geometric sections but this impression of weightiness is relieved by duck-egg blue walls with painted panels of arabesque scrolls. Furnishings here include an oak gate-leg table and balloon-back chairs as well as a pretty glass chandelier and metal wall sconces. Heating is provided by a large open fireplace.

A corner of the dining room is given over to the staircase leading to the first floor drawing room, the focal point of High Hall. This is not just owing to the panoramic views over the surrounding countryside available from various windows, but also because the room's internal prospect is so very enticing. Once more the

Dodd understands better than most the passage of time and High Hall reflects this comprehension.

OPPOSITE AND ABOVE: The magnificent four-poster in the main bedroom was designed by Alan Dodd around a piece of seventeenth-century scrollwork embroidery, probably Italian or Portuguese in origin. The late nineteenth-century metal wall

sconces are covered in decorative porcelain flowers.

RIGHT: The half-tiled bathroom with coved ceiling and an unusual ball cornice features a roll-top bath and a chaise percée incorporating a painted Mendlesham chair.

LEFT: The walls of the entrance corridor are hung with carefully pieced-together remnants of printed linen designed for the Houses of Parliament by Sir Giles Gilbert Scott. The oak-grained panelled ceiling is an allusion by Dodd to Sir Walter Scott's Abbotsford House.

OPPOSITE: In the tented bedroom, framed landscape prints cover the walls and surround a pair of giltwood wheat ear sconces. The mahogany bachelor bed and cabinets date from the first half of the nineteenth century, as does the small dressing table of simulated bamboo (see left).

ceiling is sectioned by plaster moulded beams, with the addition of a heavy ornamental cornice immediately beneath. The 'panelling' covering the walls demonstrates Dodd's trompe l'oeil skills since the impression of deep coral woodwork is entirely achieved by paint. The room's sense of formality is enhanced by the suite of armless chairs covered in linen and decorated with deep fringes, and the equally decorous seventeenth-century oak and cane seating: Dodd has been known to tell guests that if they want to relax, they should go to bed.

A similar style reigns immediately outside the house where its owner has created a small formal knot garden in memory of his late mother.

As a result of his work restoring, recreating and conceiving murals, Dodd understands better than most the passage of time and High Hall reflects this comprehension. It is a capsule of the taste of past centuries as interpreted by the present owner, well aware that the process of change and decay is inevitable and inescapable.

MANOR HOUSES

Strictly speaking, a manor house is the main dwelling on an estate owned, if not always occupied, by the lord of the manor. However, for the past few centuries, a manor house is more likely to have been the residence of a member of the landed gentry or even an affluent farmer rather than of the titled aristocracy. Neither as large nor as heavily fortified as were castles, early manor houses might have been equipped with some defensive features such as moats or ditches, but from the early sixteenth century onwards they assumed the quirky character and appearance with which we are now familiar.

OPPOSITE: The rear of the house, including its yard and outbuildings, has been transformed in recent years thanks to extensive planting as well as the addition of such elements as the authentic gypsy caravan sold by a friend to Sasha Schwerdt on condition that it be properly restored.

LEFT: Approached through a line of hazel wigwams festooned with runner beans and nasturtiums, the farm's extensive fruit and vegetable garden provides much of what is needed for lunch beneath a cluster of damson and pear trees that offer the meal's closing course.

BELOW: The plain front of the old farmhouse, its entrance flanked by a pair of hornbeams. Door and windows had to be replaced during restoration.

MANOR FARM
SOMERSET

A freelance stylist and interior decorator, over a twelve-year period prior to her marriage Sasha Schwerdt was an art director for Laura Ashley. Subsequently she spent some time working in the areas of film, book design and advertising, as well as co-founding a business called From Somewhere, which redesigned second-hand clothes to give them a new life. All of which experience has proven invaluable since 2002, the year she and her husband Simon began the painstaking process of restoring a Somerset farmhouse and its assorted outbuildings such as barns, stables and cow byres.

During the first couple of years, much of their attention and funds went on the surrounding land where hedges were planted and woods restocked. Now the farm is a model of its kind, the outbuildings looking almost too smart for the animals fortunate enough to be housed in them. Meanwhile, a substantial fruit and vegetable garden has been created behind the main house.

The old flagstones had been covered in liquid linoleum and its removal was a painfully laborious task.

Both decorative and functional, its produce not only ensures the Schwerdt family is self-sufficient but also leaves enough surplus to supply local hotels and restaurants.

Indeed, the exterior of the farm gives an excellent sense of what lies indoors. Schwerdt's impeccable eye means no detail has been overlooked. She designed the wooden gate leading from the back of the house into the vegetable garden so that its inverted curve would mirror the rose-covered arch immediately behind and thus create a perfect sphere. Nothing is wasted: wigwams to support climbing sweet peas, runner beans and nasturtiums are made from lengths of hazel coppiced from the woods, while

ABOVE AND OPPOSITE: Presided over by Border terrier Tatty, the back hall has been panelled in oak by the Schwerdts. Used for storing old coats and boots, the latter are accommodated in a sequence of old apple boxes turned on their sides. Likewise on a table by the window a French bottle rack is now used for holding keys, dog leads, torches and similar items. The toy helter-skelter beside it lights up at night. The centre table holds a vase of marigolds from the garden and a Jacobs sheep skull from the farm.

ABOVE LEFT AND RIGHT: **Inside the former porch converted into a small scullery, Winnie, a Border-cross-Lakeland terrier, surveys the abundance of produce from Manor Farm's vegetable garden. A Victorian pump and medieval well testify to the antiquity of the house. Inside the adjacent room, once used for storing coal, the Schwerdts have installed a stone sink; the door to the rear here leads to a cold room which acts as a giant refrigerator for meat, game and eggs.**

RIGHT AND OPPOSITE: **In the dining room, one wall containing a boxed-in staircase has been painted by artist Adam Calkin and the Schwerdts' daughter, Eloise. The design is based on two fragments of old painted wood brought back from Galicia, Spain. The large hearth was originally a bread oven and the table was made to be used by seamstresses: it still has measuring marks down the sides. The many kilims and fabrics scattered throughout the room were collected on travels through Turkey, India and Morocco.**

frames for the garden's raised beds recycle old windows removed from the front of the house during its restoration. Marigolds, grown as companion plants amidst the vegetables since insects flock to them first, grow in such abundance that during the summer the house is filled with bunches of the yellow and orange flowers. No better example of her inexhaustible imagination can be found than the creation of a 'magic carpet' on which sit the garden table and benches: the main part of this is made from bricks arranged in a herringbone pattern with roofing tiles around the sides cut to look like tassels and small pieces of terracotta drain to mimic the carpet's knots.

THIS PAGE AND OPPOSITE: The library-cum-study faces south and during the winter is therefore one of the warmest rooms in the house. Around its distemper-painted walls are bookcases holding a collection of children's literature and a nineteenth-century Irish pine dresser still retaining its original colour. Among the pictures is one hanging between window and door painted by Sasha's mother June de Stroumillo, showing the artist with her grandchildren.

Precise date of construction must remain a matter of conjecture – a well to the rear of the building is medieval – but the present house appears to date primarily from the early eighteenth century.

At the heart of the farm stands the main house, of two storeys and with a thatched roof. The precise date of construction must remain a matter of conjecture – a well to the rear of the building is medieval – but the present form appears to date from the early eighteenth century. While the front was finished in dressed local limestone and therefore remained unadorned, the rear walls incorporated a mixture of materials and were accordingly painted; during the course of their refurbishment the Schwerdts found fragments of a terracotta colour and so this was used for a wash over the back of the house.

Inside, some elements of the original building had survived better than others. The room now serving as a library-cum-study had been given a wooden floor but the Schwerdts discovered six inches of water beneath it. Elsewhere on the ground floor the old flagstones had been covered in liquid linoleum so as to make the surface more level and better able to take carpet; removing this material to allow the flags to be seen once more was a painfully laborious task. Actually the entire project was a protracted affair, no doubt in part due to Sasha Schwerdt's exacting personal standards. Every window

Much of the furniture has either been found in local auctions or has come from one of their parents.

had to be replaced, with proper leaded lights and oak frames, and likewise shutters were either cleaned or replaced where missing. The house was restored from the top down, which of course was the correct approach but meant that for daily living the family were confined for several years to one room, now the kitchen. At the time this was only half its present size, since the front section – today occupied by glass-fronted cabinets and a comfortable dining area – was then two small rooms: only once a couple of walls had been taken down did the kitchen as it exists today come into being. Likewise, most of the rooms were heated by little fireplaces; when

THIS PAGE AND OPPOSITE: Like most of the ground floor, the drawing room has kept its flagged floor, made from Blue Lias, a limestone still quarried locally. When the Schwerdts bought Manor Farm, the floor had been covered in liquid linoleum which had to be carefully removed. Likewise the fireplace, although it had always been in the room, had to be uncovered during the course of restoration. In addition to the Andy Warhol images of Marilyn Monroe, the room contains a small oil on canvas of roses by English painter John da Costa (1867–1931) and a set of silkscreen prints by Sasha's father, Rik de Stroumillo.

OPPOSITE AND LEFT: The kitchen today bears little similarity with its appearance when the Schwerdts first came to Manor Farm when it was three small and rather dark rooms. A small coal fire, for example, stood where the Aga now occupies pride of place inside the refurbished hearth.

ABOVE LEFT AND RIGHT: The kitchen is rightly dominated by this massive dresser, discovered in a reclamation yard and so large that it had to be cut down. Above a hook holding bags and baskets is a painting by June de Stroumillo of a bowl of fruit.

the Schwerdts removed these, they discovered, and reinstated, the generously ample hearths beneath.

If not quite a sleeping beauty, the house as the Schwerdts found it was certainly a study in dormant opportunity. Now, on the other hand, it revels in possibilities realised and all the decisions taken to reconfigure spaces and realign layouts look so right it is hard to conceive the property could ever have appeared otherwise. A small back porch containing the medieval well, along with a fine cast iron Victorian pump, has been enclosed which not only creates another useful space but also means the former coal room can now be reached without having to go outdoors.

One of the attic bedrooms follows the pitched line of the roof. The dressing table mirror by the window was a present from Simon Schwerdt's mother while the floor is covered with sheepskins from the farm.

INSET: An antique Swedish marriage box sits on a painted chest of drawers. Above it is one of Sasha Schwerdt's own paintings, a still life study inspired by the work of Giorgio Morandi, 'done when I was teaching myself about the effect of light.'

On the chimneypiece in the master bedroom sit two pictures picked up at auction while the painted cupboard to the right was bought from a local dealer. The armchair is smothered in blankets acquired at a Salvation Army sale for £1 each, while the low stool's needlepoint was stitched by Sasha Schwerdt's Russian grandfather.

LEFT: A view of the master bedroom. The bed's headboard was painted by Sasha and Eloise Schwerdt while the sofa at its feet is covered in old shawls. The curtains in this room came from a friend who designs printed velvet.

BELOW AND OPPOSITE: In the adjacent principal bathroom, the original wide elm floorboards have survived for more than 200 years as has the beam over the bath. The window sill is lined with a collection of eighteenth-century glass pharmacy bottles.

Extensive travels around the world means the house is filled with fabrics and rugs picked up in different locations. Much of the furniture has either been found in local auctions or on the premises of London dealers, or else has come from a parent. Both Sasha Schwerdt's mother and father, June and Rik de Stroumillo, paint and examples of their work are found throughout the house. Meanwhile the Schwerdts' daughter Eloise, having completed a sculpture course at Camberwell College of Art in London and helped with the decoration of the house, now freelances as a stylist in London.

Even after all this time, when other owners would be content to enjoy the fruits (and vegetables) of their labours, work on the house and its grounds continues, not least because Sasha Schwerdt is indefatigable in coming up with additional ways to ensure this farm becomes ever more a model of its kind.

BARROW FARM

HERTFORDSHIRE

The county of Hertfordshire lies immediately north of London and derives its name from the Saxon *heort ford*, meaning deer crossing. The title was first bestowed on the region following the construction of a fortress at the county town of Hertford in 913, during the rule of Edward the Elder.

But even before this event, thanks to its proximity to London and excellent agricultural land, Hertfordshire was an area of significance; in the course of the period of Roman occupation during the first centuries AD, one of its towns Verulamium – now known as St Albans – grew into the third-largest urban centre in Britain. Following the departure of the Romans and the advent of Anglo-Saxon rule, Hertfordshire became part first of the short-lived Kingdom of Essex and then of the Kingdom of Mercia. Its importance is attested by the presence of large barrows across the county. These mark the location of burial sites for leading members of Saxon society. Located less than ten miles east of Hertford town one such mound was initially a Roman fort before being adapted for interment by the Saxons and today provides an explanation for the name of nearby Barrow Farm.

For over some forty years this property has served as a weekend retreat for former Olympic skier Baron Piers von Westenholz. Situated within the acreage of a larger

OPPOSITE AND INSET: In the grounds of Barrow Farm a small summerhouse overlooks a pond where, according to von Westenholz, all the plants sowed themselves over the course of eighteen months.

RIGHT: In the corner of the garden, chickens, 'but not some obscure breed', provide the house with eggs for breakfast.

FAR RIGHT (TOP): A large barn which has always stood on the same spot was given a make-over with a wash of colour and the addition of a Pennsylvanian Hex sign.

FAR RIGHT (CENTRE): Deer antlers hang over the main entrance to the house approached by a line of hawthorn.

FAR RIGHT (BOTTOM): One of von Westenholz's alterations to the grounds has been the planting of an avenue of pleached limes.

LEFT: In the drawing room, von Westenholz installed a marble chimneypiece of his own design, inspired by the work of influential Regency designer and collector Thomas Hope. Above it sits a large Regency overmantle mirror which came from Belton House, Lincolnshire.

ABOVE: A pair of marble busts of late eighteenth-early nineteenth-century worthies sit atop antique plinths of scagliola, a composite substance made from selenite chips and designed to imitate marble.

farm then belonging to his parents, the house initially comprised two workers' cottages dating from around 1800. For the first decade and a half, they were left untouched, at least as regards their external appearance. However, once married and with children to accommodate, von Westenholz found it necessary to increase the house's dimensions, first in 1979 and again in 1985.

Previously a simple rectangle, the house is now U-shaped and some three times its original size, with one wing intended for offspring and one for guests, and the central section providing von Westenholz and his wife Jane

with a drawing room, bedroom and bathroom. Loathe to engage in self-aggrandisement – he once described himself as 'Britain's best-kept secret' – he refers to Barrow Farm as a 'glorified bungalow' although it is clearly much more than that and provides an admirable introduction to his eclectic flair. The late art historian John Cornforth, a major influence on changes in attitude towards the interior decoration of historic houses, once described von Westenholz as 'an improver of English taste in the twentieth century'. It is a task to which he has quietly but resolutely applied himself for more than forty years

THIS PAGE: An overview of the drawing room shows a large nineteenth-century oil view of Loch Tay in Perthshire where von Westenholz used to have a house. On the table before it stands a Parian ware figure of a Highland chieftain. Closer to the centre of the room is a substantial neo-classical urn and base made by the Garnkirk Fireclay Company, while to the immediate left of the door stands a model of the thirteenth-century Qutub Minar in Delhi, India.

OPPOSITE: Above the entrance hall fireplace hangs the skull and antlers of an Irish elk, beneath which is a case holding an Edwardian plastercast model of a 50lb salmon made by Mallock of Perth.

LEFT: An architectural model of a Greek temple portico stands on a chest in the hall. To the immediate right hang a series of Irish archaeological watercolours.

BELOW: In the guest wing, a corridor is entirely lined with prints of work of nineteenth-century painter and sculptor Sir Edwin Henry Landseer (1802–1873), especially renowned for his depiction of animals.

houses, is curious about how people live in them and knows how to compose their contents for a stylish and convenient way of life.'

These aspects of his character come to the fore in the way he has approached the decoration of Barrow Farm, the outcome achieving the rare feat of being simultaneously stylish and comfortable. Every room is crammed with furniture, pictures and bibelots yet nowhere looks excessively full. Likewise, although he has mixed pieces from different periods and places around the world, nothing looks out of place or ill-considered. On

The result works as smoothly as a well-rehearsed theatre ensemble.

by means of both successive London antiques outlets and a wealth of decorating commissions for English houses such as Madresfield Court, the Eythrope Pavilion, Tyringham Hall, Wilton House and Whittington Hall, as well as properties in Russia, South Africa and France. Leading decorator David Mlinaric, a long-standing friend and former business partner with whom he once shared premises on London's Lower Sloane Street, has commented of von Westenholz, 'he loves

the contrary, despite its diverse origins the finished result works as smoothly as a well-rehearsed theatre ensemble.

Of Austrian and Scottish parentage, von Westenholz brings a cosmopolitan, urbane approach to the decoration of his home where arrangements initially suggest a casual attitude but then reveal themselves to have been carefully assessed for best effect. In the drawing room, for example, note the way in which the customary horizontal lines of furniture in the centre of the space are broken up by the intervention of equally authoritative verticals, the latter provided by not only frequent features such as standard lamps but also more unusual items like a large Garnkirk urn which, like the scale model of the thirteenth-century Qutub Minar tower in India would, to a more timid eye, look both too big and strange for a domestic interior. The same ability to see beyond the obvious occurs in every room, the entrance hall typically contains both the antlers of an Irish elk and a model of a Greek temple portico as well as a collection of terracotta hare's masks made in France.

Barrow Farm's exterior provides further evidence of von Westenholz's decorating panache, not least in the application of a render to the building's walls to make them look as though made of stone. The surface has then been covered with trellis run in straight uprights rather than the more customary diagonal pattern; over this has been trained a Guinée climbing rose with deep red flowers.

Von Westenholz has rigorously limited his palette throughout the gardens to red and dark

OPPOSITE AND RIGHT: Barrow Farm's kitchen contains an overspill of watercolours and oil paintings that could not find a place elsewhere, together with a miscellany of chairs and tables. Above is an unusual geometric tongue-and-groove wooden ceiling designed by von Westenholz.

'He loves houses, is curious about how people live in them and knows how to compose their contents for a stylish and convenient way of life.'

green. Thus the pathway around the house is in brick laid in different elaborate patterns, while a brick obelisk has been covered in a climbing *Hydrangea petiolaris*. Even the old barn has been painted a deep red before a Hex symbol derived from Pennsylvania Dutch folk art was added onto the gable end. Elsewhere in the grounds he has planted avenues of lime and walnut but takes no credit for the verdant surroundings of the garden's pond, insisting 'it all happened on its own, the whole thing was self-sown in about a year and a half.' One suspects this comment to be another instance of von Westenholz's inclination towards self-effaciveness and that the pond's planting was as carefully designed as everything else at Barrow Farm. The entire property demonstrates how well he has mastered the art of apparent artlessness.

Von Westenholz brings a cosmopolitan, urbane approach to the decoration of his home where arrangements initially suggest a casual attitude.

LEFT: Still more pictures can be found in one of the house's bathrooms. Those above the length of the bath are by decorator Nicky Haslam and show interiors of von Westenholz's house in Scotland. The picture over the head of the bath is by Linda Heathcoat-Amory.

ABOVE: A William IV four-poster bed dominates one of the guest rooms. It is hung with an Indian fabric designed by the French company Pierre Frey. At the foot of the bed is an eighteenth-century carved ebony chair originally from India.

THIS PAGE: In another of the guestrooms, the bed is covered in a border check print from Pierre Frey. Above the chimney hangs a large nineteenth-century print of Lord Middleton with his Clumber spaniels. Next to it is a profile portrait of one of von Westenholz's Scottish ancestors.

OPPOSITE: When Charles Moss and John Stevenson first acquired Bramfield Folly, it had been divided by an earlier owner into three residential units, one in the basement and two sharing the ground and upper storeys. Their initial task was therefore to convert the house back into single occupancy.

RIGHT AND FAR RIGHT: Prior to restoration, the entrance hall was split by a dividing wall and contained two staircases. All this had to be removed and replaced by the present arrangement. The entrance door wall is painted with a mural by artist Nicholas Addison representing Summer; it was originally intended to be part of a larger series on the Four Seasons covering the entire hall.

BELOW: In the entrance hall, an early nineteenth-century marble-topped console table carries two painted lamps of the same period. The large oil hanging above is a portrait from Charles Moss's maternal family.

BRAMFIELD FOLLY
SUFFOLK

Once part of the Kingdom of East Anglia as its name indicates, Suffolk (Sudfole, Suthfolc, meaning 'southern folk') covered the southern region of this territory. With the North Sea lying to its east, the county is predominantly low-lying and until systematic drainage work in the seventeenth century much of it was given over to marshland and bogs. Nevertheless, the area was always populated and developed, in part due to its fishing ports but also thanks to a widespread cloth-weaving industry during the Middle Ages. In the post-drainage era when previously alluvial land was turned into arable, Suffolk became a profitable agricultural county.

E vidence of these centuries of prosperity can be seen in the abundant handsome old churches found throughout the county. Notable among these is St. Andrew's in the east Suffolk village of Bramfield: a fourteenth-century building that entirely replaced an older Norman structure, its present exterior notable for being entirely thatched. Inside survives a superb carved and gilded gesso-decorated late fifteenth-early sixteenth-century rood screen with contemporaneous painted images of saints at its base. The other distinctive feature of St. Andrew's is the freestanding round tower in the graveyard. Such towers are found across East Anglia but they are usually attached to a church and not separate from it as in this case, unique to Suffolk.

Like many buildings in this part of England, the tower of St. Andrew's – and indeed the church, too, beneath its present plaster render – is made of flint rubble with red

brick detailing. Flint is commonplace in Suffolk, found in fields which would have to be cleared of loose stones if they were to be worked; hence the recycling as a building material.

Not far from St. Andrew's, flint was extensively used in the construction of Bramfield Folly. The precise details of this house's origins are unknown. Dated by East Anglian historian Norman Scarffe as having been built at some point between 1790 and 1810, this proposal was subsequently confirmed by the late Sir Hugh Casson. However, it may occupy the site of an earlier property since there is an adjacent

ABOVE: The pink colour of the drawing room walls was copied from the dust jacket of Sir Kenneth Clark's first book, *The Gothic Revival*. Above the Knole sofa, covered in Brunschwig & Fils fabric, hangs a collection of late seventeenth- and eighteenth-century portraits in their original gilt frames. As elsewhere in the house, the original Gothick decorative features, such as this door frame, had to be rediscovered by the present owners during their programme of restoration.

OPPOSITE: Much of the drawing room's decorative detailing was installed by Charles Moss and John Stevenson, working with the artist George Galitzine, the latter responsible for the gothic cornice and ceiling rose as well as the pelmets which are made of painted fibreglass.

seventeenth-century barn and cottage. Reputedly the funds to pay for the present house came from rent money and materials purloined by an estate bailiff. Who this person might have been is unknown; a number of important families lived in the area, such as the Rabetts at nearby Bramfield Hall and the Nelsons, so it may have been one of their employees or more likely somebody working for an absentee landlord.

Even if criminal in behaviour, whoever was responsible for the building of Bramfield Folly deserves to be redeemed by his good taste. On the other hand the house's charms, so apparent today, were less in evidence when it came into the possession of Charles Moss and

Much of the house's appeal stems from its enchanting decoration.

John Stevenson some forty years ago. Then living in the Westminster district of London, the pair had decided they wanted a weekend retreat outside the capital and spent a considerable amount of time looking elsewhere in the south of England before coming to this part of the country. On first sight, Bramfield Folly was not promising. Semi-derelict, at some earlier point it had been converted from a single residence into accommodation for three

families, one in the basement and two on the ground and upper floors. Inside there were only cold water taps and outside all the woodland had been felled for timber during the Second World War. The perimeter walls were in a state of near-collapse and the original entrance flanked by matching Gothick lodges had gone. So too had the drive to the house, while the pond was in need of excavation. Littered with abandoned machinery, the rest of the grounds were given over to pigs and geese. 'But it had land,' says Charles Moss, 'and we could see the potential.'

Among the most notable elements of the house's restoration was the reinstatement of its windows. The red brick arches had been filled in with flint rubble and held small casements. These

LEFT, ABOVE AND OPPOSITE: Because a return on the main stairs cuts into a corner of the dining room ceiling, John Stevenson had the idea of covering the latter in fabric, in the tented style made fashionable in the early nineteenth century. His late father can be seen in the mid-1920s oil portrait hanging above the elegant mahogany sideboard. This item is believed to have been made by influential Regency furniture designer George Smith, as are the set of chairs; the dining table is late eighteenth century, while the carpet dates from the 1880s. The room holds part of the household's impressive collection of antique glass decanters.

OPPOSITE AND RIGHT: The breakfast room to the rear of the house has a Gothick cornice painted by Billy Dix, who also maintains the property and surrounding grounds. In the same style, the mahogany chairs with their gothic arched backs are a set of four dating from the 1840s. The large Swedish dresser filling much of one wall has kept its original decoration and is crammed with antique blue-and-white china, as are the shelves of a neighbouring recess.

were opened up once more and the present sash glazing installed and Gothick fanlights, along with the brick castellation along the roofline. The half-glazed front door was likewise created together with a flight of eight stone steps to the new entrance, surrounded on three sides by gravel terraces.

Inside the house, because of the division between different occupants, there were no less than seven staircases, all of which were taken out and replaced by the single one seen today. Gothick architraves were discovered behind the hall plaster and double doors made to the main reception rooms.

Much of the appeal of Bramfield Folly stems from its enchanting decoration. The two owners cite William Beckford, Horace Walpole and John Fowler as their principal influences, to which one might add Oliver Messel, the mid-twentieth-century artist and stage designer. A playfulness similar to his own sensibility can be seen in such elements as the tented dining room and the mural of summer inside the entrance hall; painted by Nicholas Addison, this was originally intended to be part of a larger scheme covering the Four Seasons. The drawing room's Gothick spirit is greatly enhanced by the work here of artist George Galitzine, responsible not only for the cornice and ceiling rose but also the curtain pelmets which beneath their paint are made of fibreglass. Further decoration and artwork has been painted by Billy Dix, who also maintains the property and the grounds.

Those grounds also look quite different to their former neglected state. The garden wall

THIS PAGE: Once a small bedroom, like everywhere else in the house this first-floor study is filled with books, pictures and bric-a-brac.

OPPOSITE: Another of Billy Dix's painted cornices runs around the walls of this bedroom with its late nineteenth-early twentieth-century arched mahogany bedhead, believed to have come from Heal's. The chest at the bed's foot was painted by a friend for Charles Moss's birthday.

was rebuilt and flinted, a flag terrace installed to the north of the house, the pond excavated and increased in proportions, the 14-acre parkland extensively planted with trees and 120 species of roses, and the orchard re-stocked. To the rear, a three-tier terraced courtyard was created leading to the old cottage, also restored and refenestrated with windows rescued from Bramfield's demolished eighteenth-century almshouses.

Despite all they have already achieved, the owners entertain further plans for the place, including the conversion of their barn into a music studio and concert space and the creation of a gated entrance to replace that lost before their arrival. The restoration of Bramfield Folly is not yet complete.

THIS PAGE: The late eighteenth-century four-poster bed dominating this room is hung with French silk. The large eighteenth-century portrait is in the style of George Romney while the Bargello needlework cushions and bell pull were stitched by John Stevenson.

OPPOSITE: To the right of the mid-eighteenth-century four-poster bed hung with silk damask is a painting of a dog by noted specialist in this genre Maude Earl (1864–1943).

RESTORATION HOUSE
KENT

Rochester in Kent is known to have been Charles Dickens' favourite city, since he had spent some happy time in the area as a child and in prosperous adulthood returned to buy a nearby property, eighteenth-century Gads Hill House. It is not surprising, therefore, that Rochester appears several times in fictional guise in the novelist's work, beginning with *The Pickwick Papers* in 1836 and ending with *The Mystery of Edwin Drood*, left unfinished at the time of Dickens' death in 1870. In between came *Great Expectations* featuring the unhappy spinster Miss Havisham and her decaying mansion Satis House, described as being made of 'old bricks, and dismal, and had a great many iron bars to it. Some of the windows had been walled up; of those that remained, all the lower were rustily barred'.

Although Dickens wrote of Satis House falling into ruins after Miss Havisham's death, the Rochester property believed to have been its inspiration still survives. Restoration House stands in the centre of the city, although when first built no doubt it was surrounded by open fields and gardens. Quite when work began on the property has been the subject of considerable investigation and while the absence of primary documentation means no categorical conclusions can be reached, it would appear that at least part of the core dates back to the mid-fifteenth century.

OPPOSITE: A dividing wall of 1704, but later breached, was rebuilt by the present owners in 1996 to create the 'double walled garden'. The massive chimneystack was likewise rebuilt having been subject to Victorian truncations. The result is a rear elevation as iconic as the famous facade.

LEFT: With its dramatic sequence of Dutch-inspired chimneys and gables, the powerful irregularity of Restoration House's facade dating from around 1630 caught Charles Dickens' imagination and inspired his description of Miss Havisham's home in *Great Expectations*.

ABOVE: The iron gates of c. 1700 were inserted by a Victorian owner as part of a restoration and aggrandisement programme. Restored once more, they now await their final colour.

ABOVE LEFT: The panelling in the Oak Saloon appears always to have been painted. The present colour scheme of French grey dates from the time of Charles II's visit to the house in May 1660 and has been recovered by the process of dry scraping. The gilt wood chair, one of a pair, dates from George II's reign.

ABOVE RIGHT: The south wall of the same room was re-panelled in pine in the first half of the eighteenth century, covering up the original mullion window. It is hung with a series of English portraits including a Gainsborough of his brother-in-law in the centre and a Reynolds of his friend the Rev. Zachariah Mudge to the right.

LEFT: Examples of japanning are found in various guises throughout the house, here on a George II mirror-front bookcase. The engraving is after Raphael.

OPPOSITE: The elaborately carved and fretted Elizabethan oak chimneypiece is the focus of the Oak Saloon. The painting of the young Christ as Salvator Mundi is by Italian Renaissance master Perugino, while the upholstered furniture ranges in date from Charles II to George III.

ABOVE LEFT: Now used for dining, the high and narrow Tapestry Room is so called because of the Mortlake tapestries given by Charles II which hung here until the 1890s. In their place can now be seen an Aubusson of Theseus c.1700. The Dutch seventeenth-century chandelier is one of a number of such light fittings in brass and bronze which allow the house to look as beautiful at night as it does during the day.

ABOVE TOP RIGHT AND LOWER RIGHT: Two more views of the luminous play of light in the Great Hall which is furnished with a collection of oak and country pieces.

OPPOSITE: The effect of the Great Hall's dazzling natural light is enhanced by the original pine and elm floorboards having always been scrubbed, now to a driftwood grey and further complemented by the 20-odd coats of pure white limewash on the lime plastered ceiling and upper walls. The panelling has been returned to its original earth pigmented linseed oil paint, which adds still more translucency to create a tranquil interior reminiscent of a Vermeer painting.

LEFT: The Great Chamber which lies immediately above the Great Hall has been known as Miss Havisham's Room since the time of Dickens. The colouring of green stone and off-black reproduces a scheme of the 1680s when the framed bolection-moulded panelling was installed. The room is often used for concerts featuring the antique keyboard instruments which are part of the owners' collection, here a grand fortepiano of the 1820s. The mid-eighteenth-century English chandelier is one of the few fittings to have survived several owners and is perhaps the most desirable in the house.

OPPOSITE: The so-called Eccentric Room faces east into the garden and is an odd mix of architectural styles. The carved rococo chimneypiece dates from the 1730s and the Regency revival wallpaper – found under later layers – was sensitively exhumed. The room is smothered in eighteenth-century English creamware and saltglaze pottery although the vase holding flowers is a piece of Neapolitan Capodimonte porcelain from the 1750s. The Georgian armchairs are covered in English horsehair fabric.

In its present form, Restoration House is a three-storey, red brick property with west-facing entrance front from which two substantial wings project at the north and south ends. In appearance, the exterior suggests a construction date of early to mid-seventeenth century, a supposition aided by the house's name with its reference to the restoration to the English throne of Charles II in 1660. The king is known to have stayed overnight in the house in May of that year when travelling from Dover to London on his return after 15 years of exile in continental Europe: he was the guest of a Colonel Gibbons who was then renting the property from its owner, the Royalist supporter Francis Clerke, who was soon after knighted. Seven years later, that inveterate diarist and flirt Samuel

Pepys also visited Restoration House, describing it as 'a pretty seat' where he went 'into the cherry garden, and here did meet with a young, plain, silly shopkeeper and his wife, a pretty young woman, and I did kiss her...'.

When added to the house's name and facade, this information naturally leads to a deduction that it must be seventeenth century in origin. However, forensic

Returning from 15 years in exile, Charles II is known to have stayed in the house in May 1660.

The complex history of Restoration House's creation is evident in its internal arrangement of rooms which reflect the tastes of different eras.

archaeological research carried out during the building's recent conservation and refurbishment has indicated it is not only older but was once two structures later united by the central section of the present house. In the south wing, floor joists under what is known as the Oak Saloon can be dated to around 1454. while the north wing seems to have been built in the opening decades of the following century. Most likely with different owners and occupiers, the space between these two buildings could have been open ground, and in the late sixteenth/early seventeenth century the south wing underwent further construction work, rising to four storeys with its own stair tower. Only at some date between 1600 and 1640 was the open area filled in with the building of the Great Hall and the Great Chamber above. This in turn necessitated the creation of two new stair towers as an integral part of the entrance front at the point where the old wings met the new infill. While work on the building

THIS PAGE AND OPPOSITE: Facing east to catch the morning light, the King's Bedchamber walls are hung in gold silk damask. Immediately beneath the ceiling, the black and gold japanned cornice is part of a scheme of 1684 retrospectively celebrating Charles II's earlier visit. Above a lacquer cabinet is an autographed Lely portrait, believed to be of Charles II's most famous mistress, Barbara Villiers, Duchess of Cleveland. De-accessioned from New York's Metropolitan Museum, the Italian harpsichord dated 1658 may have been made for Queen Christina of Sweden after she abdicated and moved to Rome. The four-poster bed is hung in rare Polish needlework later applied to a striking yellow grosgrain. The posts are clad in black silk damask and the coverlet is a mixture of new and antique strawberry silks.

LEFT AND BELOW: The Spindle Gallery bathroom shows evidence of a former stairwell, or garderobe or possibly a ventilated food cupboard while the revealed livery of heavy cream is from a nineteenth-century scheme that jostles with other survivals from the house's chequered history. The room's northern light is filtered through a kindly muslin curtain.

halted during the years of the Civil War and Interregnum, it resumed post-Restoration with the addition of a substantial new staircase, panelling of rooms and so forth.

The complex history of Restoration House's creation is evident in its internal arrangement of rooms which reflect the tastes of different eras, not least the eighteenth century when the building was subdivided, and a 17-year period from 1876 when it was owned by a keen antiquary Stephen Aveling, who returned the house to single occupancy and oversaw a substantial programme of restoration. To confuse further the narrative of Restoration House's history, Aveling also installed panelling and chimneypieces from elsewhere together with carved pilasters from a seventeenth-century church reredos, and in what is now called the King's Room he painted a number of scenes from Tennyson's 'Idylls of the King'. Sadly, after his

ABOVE AND RIGHT: Again located
in the north wing, the Pink Bathroom
combines archaeological purity with
a degree of comfort and retains
a glamorous suite from the 1950s.
The lime plaster, now cleaned and
stabilised with a linseed oil and
turpentine mixture, displays a history
of many colour schemes.

departure in 1893 a two-day auction of the house's contents saw the dispersal of
items which had been there since the seventeenth century, not least a set of Mortlake
tapestries believed to have been presented by Charles II.

In 1994, Restoration House was bought by Robert Tucker and Jonathan Wilmot who
have since carried out a meticulous programme of conservation work on the building.
Thanks to their efforts, much more is known about the property's history than was
ever before the case. In addition, Tucker and Wilmot have filled the rooms with
apposite furniture and paintings, so that much of the house now looks as it would
have done during its halcyon days in the seventeenth century. Outside, the surviving
garden of just over one acre has been divided into a series of 'rooms' that likewise
reflect the house's narrative and include a cutting and vegetable garden, a Jacobean-

inspired parterre, a Portland stone pond based on the shape of a Queen Anne mirror, as well as a greenhouse made from a Victorian melon house frame and an Edwardian summerhouse.

In chapter 11 of *Great Expectations*, Satis House is described as being 'spacious and I dare say had once been handsome, but every discernible thing in it was covered with dust and mould, and dropping to pieces.' This is now far from being the case. On the contrary, as Jeremy Musson wrote in *Country Life* in July 2002, the building's present owners have 'ensured a long life for the house by major repairs and created interiors of rare historical resonance and poetry.'

ABOVE AND RIGHT: In another bedroom, the little plank door once led into the old Tudor Hall, demolished around 1700. An original mullion window, though blocked up internally, has been revealed while the ceiling bears stains of tar and flooding drawn forth by an organic limewash. The wide elm floorboards are amongst the most characterful in the house.

THIS PAGE AND OPPOSITE: Built around 1820, the house was originally two farm workers' cottages but made into a single family home at the start of the last century. As can be seen here, unusually one half of the roof is traditionally covered in local slate, the other in pantiles. Each side of the building retains its own entrance, that on the north front now distinguished by a bright red porch which replaced an older one too far dilapidated to be rescued during the restoration.

FARM HOUSE
NORTHUMBERLAND

Northumberland is England's northernmost county, as well as being the most sparsely populated: there are only some 62 people per square kilometre. Being on the border with Scotland, this part of the country was for many centuries the scene of regular conflict, hence another local statistic is that Northumberland has the largest number of castles of any English county. A large section of Hadrian's Wall also passes through here, evidence of the area's importance even in the Roman period.

Although Julius Caesar first invaded Britain in 55 BC, it was almost a hundred years later before the Emperor Claudius sent a large force to the island to establish firm control of these territories. Although the south was soon subjugated, the northern part of England and what is now the Scottish lowlands continued to cause trouble, even after further advances were made during the reign of Vespasian. So when the Emperor Hadrian visited Britain in 122 AD, he ordered a wall be built between the Solway Firth in the west and the River Tyne in the east 'to separate Romans from Barbarians'.

While the wall accomplished this task for a time, as the Roman Empire disintegrated the northern tribes once more encroached into England and this would remain the case for more than a millennium. Whoever controlled Northumberland wielded considerable power because the county served as a protective barrier against

ABOVE LEFT: A gothic-arched wooden gateway set into one of the farm's walls and, through its openings, provides views for miles across the expanse of surrounding countryside.

BELOW: Espaliered fruit trees have been trained along wire in the south-facing garden. Although strong winds blow across a moorland unbroken by belts of forestry, it has been possible to grow hardy plants here.

LEFT: In the dining room, the walls are covered in a screen-printed paper by Catherine Morris. Above the chimneypiece is an old painting of the house, bought at a local auction by the present owner.

BELOW LEFT: The sitting room is dominated by a chimneypiece from France but most of the other items are English, such as the antique gothic cabinet found at an antiques fair. The print of a dog is by Lucian Freud while the ottoman, along with most of the soft furnishings, came from designer Robert Kime.

OPPOSITE: The front door opens into a hall which appears to be floored in Victorian encaustic tiles; in fact, they are of recent manufacture and came from Morocco. The painting of Wiltshire on the end wall is by David Inshaw.

A great deal of work had to be undertaken during the house's year-long restoration with a lot of the basic fabric replaced.

battle of Flodden Field on Branxton Moor. By this time, centuries of cross-border skirmishing had led to Northumberland being notorious for lawlessness and it was only with the accession of Scotland's James VI to the English throne as James I that the county finally began to come under the authority of central government.

Later the county experienced a different kind of upheaval as it played a significant role in the Industrial Revolution; the presence of large supplies of coal in Northumberland not only led to the development of mines but also, in order to transport the coal, the creation of some of the earliest railway lines. Since the decline in mining throughout England, Northumberland has reverted to being a predominantly rural country dependent on agriculture. The disappearance of heavy industry has also meant the romance of the region's wild moorland landscape is more widely appreciated than was formerly the case. Today about a quarter of the county is largely protected from development

threatened invasion from Scotland. Based at Alnwick since the thirteenth century, the Percys, who became Earls and later Dukes of Northumberland, were the most important family in the region. By special enactment in 1382, for instance, the first Earl was ordered to remain on his estates to protect the border. Six years later his son Henry Percy, immortalised by Shakespeare as Harry Hotspur, was taken prisoner fighting against the Scots at the Battle of Otterburn. In 1513, King James IV of Scotland was slain in the

as the Northumberland National Park, an area stretching south from the Scottish border to include Hadrian's Wall.

It is precisely the unspoilt character of the Northumberland countryside that led the owner of this farmhouse to acquire the property in 2004. Situated six miles inland from the coast and not far from Alnwick, the building was originally constructed as two cottages around 1820 but is believed to have become a single dwelling at the start of the last century. One of the most distinctive features of its exterior is that half of the house's roof is covered in fired clay pantiles, the other in slate, the latter being more customary for the area. Quite why this should be the case has never been understood, the feature being even more inexplicable since the same family of sheep farmers inhabited the property from the time it was built until the 2004 sale. Surrounded by open farmland and with few other houses within sight, the site is extremely exposed to the elements and protected only by the area's traditional dry-stone walls.

A great deal of work had to be undertaken during the house's year-long restoration: its owner remembers her son standing in mud inside what is now the kitchen looking at the sky above him. That space underwent the most radical alteration since it had hitherto been a coalhole. No evidence of this function is now apparent, not least because the

ABOVE AND OPPOSITE: The kitchen was originally a coalhole and had to be entirely rebuilt during restoration, allowing a high pitched ceiling to be installed. The new oak flooring came from Wales. Many of the furnishings reflect an interest in the late nineteenth-early twentieth-century Arts and Crafts Movement; the table and chairs here, for example, are by the influential architect and designer Ernest Gimson. The colourful cups and saucers are examples of work by potter Anne Stokes, while many of the pictures on the walls were painted by the owner's children.

ABOVE: The hall's woodwork, including the staircase, was re-grained by a local craftsman during the house's restoration. Here the open door leads into a guest bedroom, with an Ikat fabric hanging behind the bed. All the chimneypieces upstairs are original to the house.

LEFT: The guest bedroom's chest of drawers was found at Battersea Antiques Fair. Above it hangs a painting of sunflowers by twentieth-century neo-romantic artist Charles Mahoney.

FAR LEFT: In the bathroom, a claw-footed bath is sited to catch an outstanding view southwards across unspoilt countryside.

The furnishings come from a diverse range of sources but most of the house's abundant pictures are by British artists.

ABOVE: The walls of a children's bedroom are covered in paper hand-printed from lino cuts by Marthe Armitage, who has been working in this field since the middle of the last century and using the same press for more than forty years. The pair of French beds came from London antique dealer Judy Greenwood.

tongue-and-groove ceiling rises some fourteen feet above the oak floorboards. Elsewhere as much as possible, the house's original features were retained, not least the main staircase which a local specialist re-grained, as he did other woodwork such as doorframes. But a lot of the basic fabric had to be replaced. The main north-facing entrance, for example, already had a glass porch but this was so badly weathered that demolition was inevitable. It was replaced with a new one, today painted a welcoming bright red.

Inside, the furnishings have come from a diverse range of sources, reflecting the owner's interests. The entrance hall tiles, for example, although they look like typical examples of Victorian encaustic work actually came from Morocco, while the sitting room's large stone chimneypiece is French. However, most of the pictures abundantly hung throughout the building are by British artists. At the moment, this house is used primarily for weekends and holidays and the owner describes it as a work in progress. With family connections in the area, her ambition is to move there permanently in the years ahead, so that the romantic surrounding Northumberland landscape can be enjoyed on a daily basis.

COUNTRY HOUSES

POPULARLY KNOWN AS 'STATELY HOMES', ENGLAND'S COUNTRY HOUSES ARE ONE OF HER GREATEST GLORIES. FREQUENTLY NEGLECTED DURING THE FIRST HALF OF THE LAST CENTURY, THEIR DISTINCTIVE NATURE HAS SINCE COME TO BE RECOGNISED AND CHERISHED, NOT LEAST BECAUSE THEY REFLECT SO MUCH THAT IS BEST OF THE COUNTRY'S HISTORY. ALTHOUGH SOME DATE FROM BEFORE THE SEVENTEENTH CENTURY, THE MAJORITY OF SUCH HOUSES WERE BUILT AFTER THE END OF THE CIVIL WAR WHEN AN ABIDING INTERNAL PEACE SETTLED ON ENGLAND AND OWNERS NO LONGER HAD TO FEAR THE THREAT OF ATTACK, HENCE THE IMPRESSION GIVEN BY ENGLAND'S COUNTRY HOUSES OF BEING COMFORTABLY AND CONFIDENTLY SETTLED IN THEIR OWN PLACE.

PORT ELIOT
CORNWALL

It has been estimated that prior to the English Reformation of the 1530s, the Catholic Church owned between one-fifth and one-third of the entire country. A major consequence of Henry VIII's subsequent seizure and disposal of all this property was that it created an entire new class of landowner, among them the Plymouth merchant adventurer John Eliot, who in 1564 bought a former Augustinian priory and its surrounding grounds some miles south of his native city.

Situated on Cornwall's Tamar Estuary, St. Germans takes its name from the fifth century St. Germanus of Auxerre and is believed to date from his visit to England around 429 AD, making it one of the country's oldest sites in continuous habitation. The church here grew in importance to become a bishop's seat and the cathedral of Cornwall. However, in 1046 the diocese was merged with that of Exeter and over a century later St. Germans was re-founded as a house of the Augustinian canons. Their large Norman church, with its two western towers and 102 feet nave, remains but

LEFT: Port Eliot's exterior still shows evidence of its original creation as an Augustinian priory. The large round tower on the extreme left of the north front, for example, occupies the site of the medieval prior's lodge while the seven first-floor windows to its immediate right were once the refectory. Until improvements made by the Eliots, water came right up to the building: a patch of red Virginia creeper marks what used to be the priory's boathouse entrance. Rising behind can be seen the mass of the Norman St. German's church.

RIGHT: The gothicised conservatory is part of Sir John Soane's early nineteenth-century alterations; the *Magnolia grandiflora*, together with several others on the south facade, is about 150 years old.

at the time of the Reformation the priory which lay to the immediate north was stripped of all valuables before being sold in 1538 to a Devon squire, John Champernowne; his son Henry in turn sold on the estate to John Eliot whose successors have lived there ever since. Previously called Porth Prior, from 1573 the property was known as Port-Elyot, and later as Port Eliot.

John Eliot's grand-nephew, also called John, was a Member of Parliament and prominent defender of its rights and privileges against the crown, declaring in the House of Commons in March 1629, 'By the ancient laws and liberties of England it is the known birthright and inheritance of the subject that no tax, tallage or other charge shall be levied or imposed but by common consent.' For this and other supposed

ABOVE LEFT: On an onyx-topped eighteenth-century Irish yew table in the lobby sits a contemporary model of the boat with which Wolfe stormed Quebec in 1759. The green wallpaper is late nineteenth century, the colour deriving from a highly toxic compound based on copper and arsenic.

ABOVE AND OPPOSITE: Once Port Eliot's main entrance, since the Soane alterations this has been the morning room. Its walls are lined with crimson French damask hung in the 1870s. The ten pictures within a baroque frame are part of Van Dyke's iconography.

LEFT: The inner hall, with its stairwell designed by Soane. The lower portrait is of John Hampden, the seventeenth-century MP who, like Sir John Eliot, resisted Charles I's efforts to rule and raise taxes without reference to Parliament.

LEFT: **Offering views across the eighteenth-century Humphrey Repton-landscaped park, the Salon's walls are hung with portraits of the Eliot family painted by Sir Joshua Reynolds. Its diverse furnishings include a Carlton House desk, eighteenth-century silver wine coolers converted into lamps and a Robert Kime sofa bought from eBay.**

Sir John Soane was responsible for creating runs of rooms.

instances of *lèse-majesté*, he was committed by Charles I to the Tower of London, dying there three years afterwards.

Later Eliots were less politically active, many of them devoting themselves to the betterment of their house and estate. Initially the family occupied the old priory buildings, of which traces still remain in the basement, but by the early eighteenth century alterations began to be undertaken to make the building more comfortable. In 1792 Edward Eliot, who had been created Baron Eliot eight years earlier, commissioned the landscape gardener Humphrey Repton to redesign the parkland, and early in the following century William Gilpin drew up plans for the improvement of the pleasure grounds. In 1804 Lord Eliot was succeeded by his son John who eleven years later became the first Earl of St. Germans. By this time the house's appearance had been radically altered thanks to the work of neo-classical architect Sir John Soane. He was responsible for creating runs of rooms in two ranges, with salon and drawing room to the north and dining room and billiard room to the south. The first earl was succeeded by his brother who in 1829 undertook further building work, notably the porte cochère and substantial service block, using as architect Henry Harrison.

'The lawns and glen which surround the mansion,' proclaimed an admirer in 1848, 'display a brilliant and never-fading verdure, over which the hanging foliage droops most luxuriously... The vale appears to enclose only the lordly mansion,

the venerable church and its two ancient towers...' This description is as apposite now as it was then.

Today Port Eliot has 13 staircases, 82 chimneys, 15 back doors (but only one front door) and a roof covering half an acre. It contains some 100 rooms but only eleven radiators. With one notable exception, little has changed for the past century and a half. 'More than the occasional thread hangs from the crimson damask-clad walls, hung in 1892 and now faded to a shade of raspberry fool,' wrote the Countess of St. Germans in 2008, 'and the carpets are probably a health and safety peril.' The significant addition to internal decoration was her husband's commissioning from Robert Lenkiewicz a mural for Soane's Round Room in the north-east corner of the house. Forty feet in diameter, the walls of this immense space are covered in work to which the artist devoted himself on and off for some thirty years and had still not completed when he died in 2002. Half the imagery depicts death, destruction, insanity, unrequited love and an apocalyptic end of the world while the rest is concerned with love, friendship, harmony, proportion and consensus. Concealed within the work are references to family skeletons, art history and cabalistic mysteries. For this reason it is known as the Riddle Mural.

If Port Eliot's appearance has scarcely altered since the mid-nineteenth century, its role has undergone something

ABOVE AND OPPOSITE: Designed by Soane, the Round Room's walls are covered in murals by the late Robert Lenkiewicz. A mid nineteenth-century 28-light French lead crystal chandelier hangs from a ceiling rose over a circular Aubusson carpet originally made for the Brighton Pavilion. A vintage Harley Davidson bike rests beside one of the windows.

of a transformation thanks to the annual literary festival held in the grounds each summer. The predecessor to this event was the Elephant Fayre, a performance festival which ran at Port Eliot for six years until 1986. In 2003, Catherine, Countess of St. Germans together with publishing director Simon Prosser, decided to start a new festival, one based around literature but with greater freedom of spirit than is usually evident at these gatherings. They invited friends – novelists, poets and journalists – to perform material unlikely to be heard at more traditional events. In its first year the festival attracted 17 paying punters, along with three times as many performers, artists and crew but since then numbers have grown and its fame spread. 'All the brains of a literary festival,' judged *The Times*, 'All the soul of a music festival.' The Augustinian canons who once occupied this site were enjoined to offer hospitality to travellers. While they might not have appreciated every aspect of the Port Eliot Festival it is fair to say the estate continues a practice with origins long predating the Reformation.

THIS PAGE AND OPPOSITE: Many centuries ago this was the priory's refectory, then later the hall and on another occasion the library; today it is the drawing room. The curved bookcase wall beyond the screen of paired Ionic columns is part of Soane's redecoration. Among the room's diverse furniture is a pair of gilt papier-mâché walls mirrors in the Chippendale style, a Japanese seventeenth-century lacquered chest, a pair of Imari vases and a large folio bookcase. Theatre designer and art director Michael Howells made the chandelier from silk flowers.

WEMBURY
DEVON

Elected Bishop of Exeter in 1107, William
Warelwast, who is believed to have been
a relative of William the Conqueror,
subsequently founded and liberally endowed
the Augustinian Priory of Plympton in Devon;
soon it was one of the richest religious houses
in that area of the country. The estate of
Wembury, which lies on the south Devon coast
not far from Plymouth Sound, became part of
Plympton's endowment and remained such
until Henry VIII's dissolution of all monastic
establishments in 1539. The lands of Wembury
were then granted by the King to Thomas
Wriothesley, first Earl of Southampton, a royal
favourite and the recipient of more than one
Devon monastic property. But his son, the
second Earl, disposed of the estate and in
1591 it was bought by Sir John Hele.

OPPOSITE: When Tim and Emma
Hanbury moved into Wembury, they
switched the axis of the house from
west to east, making what had been
the rear into the entrance front.

ABOVE RIGHT: A new door replaced
a sash window and new flights of
steps were created to descend from
entrance to garden.

RIGHT: In the hall, a model of
Wembury made by designer Freddy
van Zevenbergen sits at the foot of
the stairs which date from the early
nineteenth century.

O ne of the many lawyers who prospered
during the reign of Elizabeth I, Hele came
from a large Devon family. Within a year
of buying Wembury, he had been appointed both
MP and Recorder for Exeter and in 1594 he was
in London as a Serjeant-at-law, one of a small
elite group of barristers at the English bar. He
was promoted to Principal Serjeant by James I,
who knighted him in 1603 and that same year
it was as the King's representative that he
prosecuted another Devonian, the explorer Sir
Walter Raleigh, on charges of treason.

Sir John's legal practice made him a great
deal of money, and he spent much of it on
transforming Wembury into a princely new
residence on the site of the old monastic

building. The result was subsequently described as 'equalling if not excelling all other in these western parts for uniform building, a sightly seat for shew, for receipt spacious; for cost sumptuous; for sight, salubrious; near the sea, upon an advanced ground, whereby all houses of office are under it; having a delightful prospect both to sea and land.'

As for the interiors, an observer in 1701 wrote that the dining room chimneypiece alone was 'valued at no less than five hundred pounds containing the representation of two armies drawn up in batalia, all in polished marble, done after the life with such exactness, that nothing can exceed it; the very nails in the horseshoes are not omitted.' The cost of Sir John's house, which contained forty-two hearths – the largest number by far recorded in any house in Devon – was estimated to be twenty thousand pounds; even the gatehouse was 'fit for the accommodation for a large and genteel family'.

Yet nothing of this prodigious building survives today. Indeed, the only extant element of Sir John's residence is a vast buttressed

Wembury seems to have changed hands more than any other house in Devon.

ABOVE AND RIGHT: **Although not on the same palatial scale as its predecessor, Wembury is a substantial house, its main rooms demanding grand statements. Emma Hanbury's solution has been to find outsize pieces of furniture, such as the gilt mirror above the drawing room chimneypiece; this is matched by a second mirror on the facing wall.**

rampart on the south-west boundary of the present garden, broad enough to sustain a grass terrace. It is unclear whether its original purpose was to ensure privacy or to serve as a defence, but the proximity of the sea and the possibility of invasion suggests the latter.

Wembury seems to have changed hands more than any other house in Devon. It had done so several times by the end of the seventeenth century when it was sold to the local Member of Parliament, John Pollexfen, who had much of the place rebuilt. Further changes of ownership took

The bright drawing room occupying Wembury's south-east corner contains an elegant white marble fireplace carved with a central putto and female figures to either side. The ceiling is bordered by a fine cornice and from the ample centre rose hangs a chandelier brought from Tim Hanbury's family home in Leicestershire.

place over the next hundred years and a decade before being bought in 1803 for twenty-six thousand pounds by Plymouth merchant Thomas Lockyer, it was described as being in a state of great decay if not entirely dilapidated.

Lockyer chose to start again on the site, demolishing the old house and building another in its place, although a fatal carriage accident three years after his purchase meant he never saw the finished building. This early nineteenth-century five-bay house is of two storeys over basement (and concealed attic) and built in rubble stone with ashlar dressings.

Within twenty years Lockyer's son had sold the house and it changed hands a further six times

OPPOSITE: What had once been the house's rear hall is now the principal entrance, with drawing and dining rooms to either side. Above the door into the latter is an example of Emma Hanbury's imaginative ingenuity: sections of French fabric cut into ovals and inserted in gilt frames.

LEFT AND ABOVE: In the dining room both the table and candelabra came from Tim Hanbury's old home, while four of the chairs are eighteenth-century originals, the rest being copies. On the sideboard is a Wembury Warmer, a hotplate of Emma Hanbury's design now found in almost every English country house.

before being bought by the present owners, Tim and Emma Hanbury, in 1988. At the time Wembury was, they say, 'in a pretty bad state and rather rundown'. Among the major tasks that required undertaking was the installation of a new roof and attention to many of the windows. Since these jobs had to be done, the Hanburys took advantage of the opportunity to implement a couple of significant alterations to the house.

Firstly they realigned its axis by moving the entrance from west to east front; this involved replacing a central sash window with a door and creating a double flight of granite steps down to the garden. In addition, the Hanburys installed windows on the house's south side which, until their intervention, had been entirely blind and accordingly suffered from loss of natural light. Now on the ground floor, for example, it is possible to step out onto a terrace and from there descend into a courtyard containing an outdoor swimming pool.

Internally, Wembury is a classic double-pile house with rooms opening front and rear off a central staircase hall, and a service wing built onto the north side. Aside

ABOVE: Around papered walls above the library bookcases are hung a framed series of illuminated documents and addresses belonging to Tim Hanbury's family.

OPPOSITE: Although the bookcases are original to the house, the appearance of their shelves has been greatly improved by Emma Hanbury's addition of cut-out borders of marbleised paper.

On the first floor, the Hanburys have created four bedroom suites, including this one with its pretty floral wallpaper. Among the furnishings are an eighteenth-century painted Italian bed inherited from Emma's grandmother and a gilt rococo-style overmantle bought at a local auction.

from changing the main axis, the Hanburys made few changes to Wembury's internal structure but demonstrated flair and ingenuity in their approach to its decoration. Emma has run a clothing business for the past decade but is now spending more time involved in interior design; recently she worked with her ex-model daughter Marina, newly-married Countess of Durham, on the restyling of Biddick, County Durham. In addition, the Hanburys are responsible for the Wembury Warmer, an ingenious hotplate that can be found on sideboards in almost every English country house. By this means, the influence of Wembury has spread far beyond the borders of Devon.

LEFT: By installing windows on the south side of Wembury, the Hanburys increased the amount of light inside the house and this especially benefitted the bed- and bathrooms on the first floor, such as this one. The four-poster bed here was inherited from Emma Hanbury's mother, while the oil of children over the chimneypiece came from Antiquarius in London.

RIGHT: Handsome mahogany double doors open from a bedroom onto the upper landing, which is sufficiently spacious to accommodate sofas and a writing desk with views eastwards across the surrounding landscape. The enfilade then continues through another set of doors into a bedroom and dressing room.

BELOW RIGHT: In one of the first-floor dressing rooms, Emma Hanbury has enhanced the bed's character by the simple device of creating a semi-circular canopy over its head hung with old fabric.

The Hanburys have demonstrated flair and ingenuity in their approach to Wembury's decoration.

MAPPERTON
DORSET

A consequence of England's many centuries of internal peace is the number of houses allowed to evolve undisturbed by upheaval. Mapperton in Dorset provides an example of this happy circumstance, a property passed by inheritance from one generation to the next over some 850 years before being put on the market for the first time in 1919.

And even this event, repeated when the house was again sold in 1956, thanks to successive new owners' sympathetic understanding has providentially enhanced Mapperton's allure so that, as was written in *Country Life* in 1962, 'The whole group of buildings has an extraordinary charm and beauty of a kind that drawing-board architecture is incapable of achieving.'

The land on which Mapperton stands was entered in the Domesday Book as Malperetone. It was then the property of William de Moion, Sheriff of Somerset, who earned 70 shillings from arable land for four ploughs, twenty acres of meadow and pasture, woodlands and a mill. Thereafter the estate belonged to only four families linked by descent in the female line – the Bretts, Morgans, Brodrepps and Comptons. A member of the second of these, Robert Morgan, built the earliest extant part of the present house at Mapperton during the reign of Henry VIII. This – the north wing of honey-toned Ham Hill

LEFT: A pair of eagle-topped stone gate-piers provides access to Mapperton's entrance, which owes its present appearance to alterations made in the seventeenth and eighteenth centuries.

ABOVE LEFT: Mapperton's Hall, although built in the sixteenth century, shows the accretions of successive generations, its Jacobean overmantle having been brought from another house in 1908 and the ornamented ceiling in the 1920s.

LEFT: In the entrance passage, the south wall is covered by a Carolingian screen into which a late seventeenth-century doorway has been inserted to provide access to the dining room.

RIGHT: In the drawing room a large seascape by Samuel Scott records an incident in July 1745 when HMS *Lion* attempted to intercept a French vessel the *Elizabeth* bringing Charles Stuart, the Young Pretender, to Scotland.

Quite which member of the family commissioned changes has never been confirmed.

limestone, its gable end marked by twisted chimneys and heraldic finials – would have held the family's private quarters, the more public hall range running at right angles from the eastern corner. It might have been expected that in the fashion of the time Robert Morgan would construct an E-shaped dwelling, but he was prevented from doing so by the presence of an existing chapel to the immediate south; although the nave was rebuilt in 1704, it remains on the same site and thanks to the presence of a pair of contemporaneous gate-piers and later railings, provides Mapperton with a graceful forecourt.

By the time these additions were made, the estate had passed by marriage into the hands of the Brodrepps, one of whom was responsible for rebuilding the hall range at some point around the middle of the seventeenth century, adding such decorative details as an entrance porch, although the roofline's symmetrical balustrade is probably later again. Quite which member of the family undertook this work has never been confirmed but it was Richard Brodrepp who commissioned the two ranges of stables flanking the outer courtyard, and the square-gabled pigeon house to the immediate south. The last of the

OPPOSITE: While the drawing room's panelling and chimneypiece are eighteenth century, the plaster ceiling with repeated fleur-de-lys motif is a survivor of the original Tudor decoration.

ABOVE LEFT AND RIGHT: Around 1750 the last Richard Brodrepp to live at Mapperton oversaw the insertion of a new staircase in the centre of the north range. Above the door leading to the drawing room can be seen portraits of the fourth Earl of Sandwich and his mistress, singer Martha Ray, who was murdered in 1779 by a jealous clergyman, James Hackman.

Brodrepps to live at Mapperton, also called Richard, made further structural alterations when he had the old Tudor segment remodelled both externally and internally, with a new, sash-windowed frontage on the north side and a staircase hall inserted into the centre portion of the wing. Although, as before, the work cannot be attributed with certainty, it may have been designed by William and John Bastard, Dorset-born surveyor-architect brothers, examples of whose manner found elsewhere in the county are not dissimilar to in Mapperton's Georgian quarters.

Once this final Richard Brodrepp died in 1774, the property passed to one of his sisters' families, the Comptons who remained there until 1919. Mapperton was then sold to Mrs Ethel Labouchere who not only improved the interior of the house with the addition of Elizabethan-style ceilings in the hall and dining room but also created an elaborate garden to the east of the house with topiary, pergolas and flights of steps. This garden was further enhanced from 1956 onwards following the purchase of Mapperton by Victor Montagu, who served as Conservative MP for the area. His son, John Montagu, 11th Earl of Sandwich, is the house's present owner, and he and his wife have, in turn, further improved the property.

Like many notable English families, the Montagus rose to prominence thanks to a canny lawyer forbear during the Tudor period: from Sir Edward Montagu, appointed by Henry VIII as one of the executors of the King's last will and a governor to his son

LEFT AND ABOVE: The dining room panelling and its bolection mould chimneypiece date from an extensive remodelling of the hall range during the second half of the seventeenth century. The present ceiling, however, was one of the alterations carried out after the house passed into the ownership of Mrs Labouchere in 1919. A door in one corner of the room provides access to an antechamber leading directly into the chancel of the church that is in effect Mapperton's south wing.

Edward VI, were descended three peerages: the Dukes of Montagu; the Dukes of Manchester; and the Earls of Sandwich. The first holder of that last title, also called Edward Montagu, was an admiral in Charles II's navy, dying in 1672 at the Battle of Solebay; he was a first cousin of Samuel Pepys' father and the diarist owed his career as a naval administrator to the earl's influence. John Montagu, fourth Earl of Sandwich was likewise associated with the British navy, serving on three

LEFT: The panelling and chimney piece in the 'chapel' bedroom were remodelled by the Bastard brothers in the eighteenth century when they redesigned the staircase hall. Among the contemporary furniture are a George III four-poster bed and a Regency scroll end day-bed.

OPPOSITE AND ABOVE: The Great Chamber in the house's north-east corner contains the best of Mapperton's extant Tudor decoration, notably the plaster ribbed and pendanted ceiling and, immediately beneath, a frieze that features alternating Italianate putti and profile heads in wreaths. The contemporary overmantle incorporates the Morgan coat of arms and motto.

occasions as First Lord of the Admiralty. A keen supporter of Captain James Cook's Pacific exploration, he provided Admiralty funds for the purchase of several vessels including the *Discovery*. In return, in 1778 Cook named the Sandwich Islands – now known as Hawaii – after his patron.

Despite devoting much of his life to politics, the fourth Earl of Sandwich tends to be remembered for other reasons, not least a long affair with opera singer Martha Ray who bore him several children – raised with his legitimate offspring – before being murdered in the foyer of the Royal Opera House, Covent Garden by a jealous clergyman, James Hackman. Famously after the earl told actor Samuel Foote, 'I have often wondered what

catastrophe would bring you to your end; but I think, that you must either die of the pox, or the halter,' he met with the response, 'My lord, that will depend upon one of two contingencies: whether I embrace your lordship's mistress, or your lordship's principles.'

Lord Sandwich is credited with first requesting the meal that still bears his name: the sandwich. Though its origins have been the subject of much debate for more than two centuries, the tale is often told that the earl, while at either the gaming table or his desk, asked a valet to bring him some meat tucked between two pieces of bread. Other men subsequently started to request 'the same as Sandwich', hence the name came into common circulation.

LEFT: A large section of the 'ruins' of Euridge Manor comes from stone quarried on the site when the gardens were being created. Here a large wall of mostly uncut stone is smothered in climbing roses; in front of it stands a gypsy caravan sometimes used for tea by Belle Robinson.

RIGHT: A series of pools runs along the length of the upper terrace in front of the orangery.

FAR RIGHT: The new entrance of the house is one of its most recent additions, as can be seen by the colour of the stone which only mellows to honey tones after a few years.

EURIDGE MANOR
WILTSHIRE

Gothic ruins have been a feature of the English landscape ever since the dissolution of the country's monasteries by Henry VIII from 1539 onwards. Owing to ongoing religious disputes between different Christian sects, for a long time these decaying structures were regarded with little favour. But by the eighteenth century, when the country had become more stable, the buildings' romantic allure began to be recognised. Ruined Cistercian abbeys were especially prized for their beauty, those of Rievaulx and Fountains in Yorkshire, for example, becoming centrepieces of formally laid-out parks. Further south on the Welsh border, Tintern Abbey was not only commemorated in 1798 in a poem by William Wordsworth but some fifteen years later an engraving of its ruins is mentioned in Jane Austen's *Mansfield Park.*

Since monastic ruins were not always conveniently sited or could be excessively dilapidated, it was not long before a fashion arose to create new ones, often with accommodation. A vogue for the gothic style, known at the time as 'Gothick', was popularised by the likes of Horace Walpole, son of Prime Minister Sir Robert Walpole, who in 1749 started to build for himself a neo-gothic villa, Strawberry Hill in Twickenham, not far from London.

The attraction of ruins has never entirely disappeared and explains the transformation of Euridge Manor.

There was nothing purist about this approach to decoration and gothic details were often mixed with elements of rococo and chinoiserie.

In 1795 William Beckford, known as the richest commoner in England, began work on the construction of an immense new home, Fonthill Abbey, on his estate in Wiltshire. Although entirely newly-built to the designs of architect James Wyatt, the abbey was intended to look as if dating back to the Middle Ages. However, the loss of much of his income in the early 1820s forced Beckford to sell the property and within a few years Fonthill's main tower had collapsed, much of the rest of the structure

ABOVE LEFT: In a corner of the garden stands a castellated squat tower offering views of the countryside from its battlements.

ABOVE: The terrace outside the drawing room looks down on the pool which concludes with an elaborately thatched boathouse.

OPPOSITE: Evoking the ripely planted gardens of England's Edwardian era, that at Euridge is filled with a wide variety of flowering roses interspersed with clipped box and yew cones.

Despite such decorative details as the ornate cornice, Euridge's main drawing room is less than ten years old. Used for entertaining, it holds a finely carved antique fireplace, above which rests a nineteenth-century oil painting of a Mrs Robinson, no relation of the present owners. Their two daughters play the grand piano standing in the far bay of the room.

being subsequently demolished. Ironically today for architectural historians, it is a place of romantic pilgrimage.

By the time of Fonthill's collapse, a more architecturally-authentic Gothic Revival was underway both in England and elsewhere in Europe and remains of medieval buildings were cherished in a way that had not previously been the case. But the attraction of ruins has never entirely disappeared and explains the transformation in recent years of Euridge Manor in Wiltshire.

At its core the house dates back several centuries. In fact, owner John Robinson says he believes it was originally a hunting lodge belonging to Sir Walter Raleigh. But by the time he bought the place in 1980 it looked like a regular Victorian farm, neither very substantial nor especially distinguished. His own romantic instincts are apparent in the successful business he founded with a partner in 1972: the women's clothing company Jigsaw. Initially he and his wife

THIS PAGE: In the family room, the stone fireplace was, says John Robinson, 'cobbled together from a variety of different bits.'

OPPOSITE: The same room's large painted dresser was likewise constructed from different elements, although its upper section is old.

Belle did not undertake much structural work on the house, which lies at the centre of a working farm. The couple only decided to expand their rural retreat in 1999 and called on the services of long-standing friends and noted garden designers Julian and Isabel Bannerman. 'I'd seen how they'd created a ruin around their swimming pool,' John explains, 'and asked them to do something similar for me. But then Julian came back and told me our swimming pool was in the wrong place…'

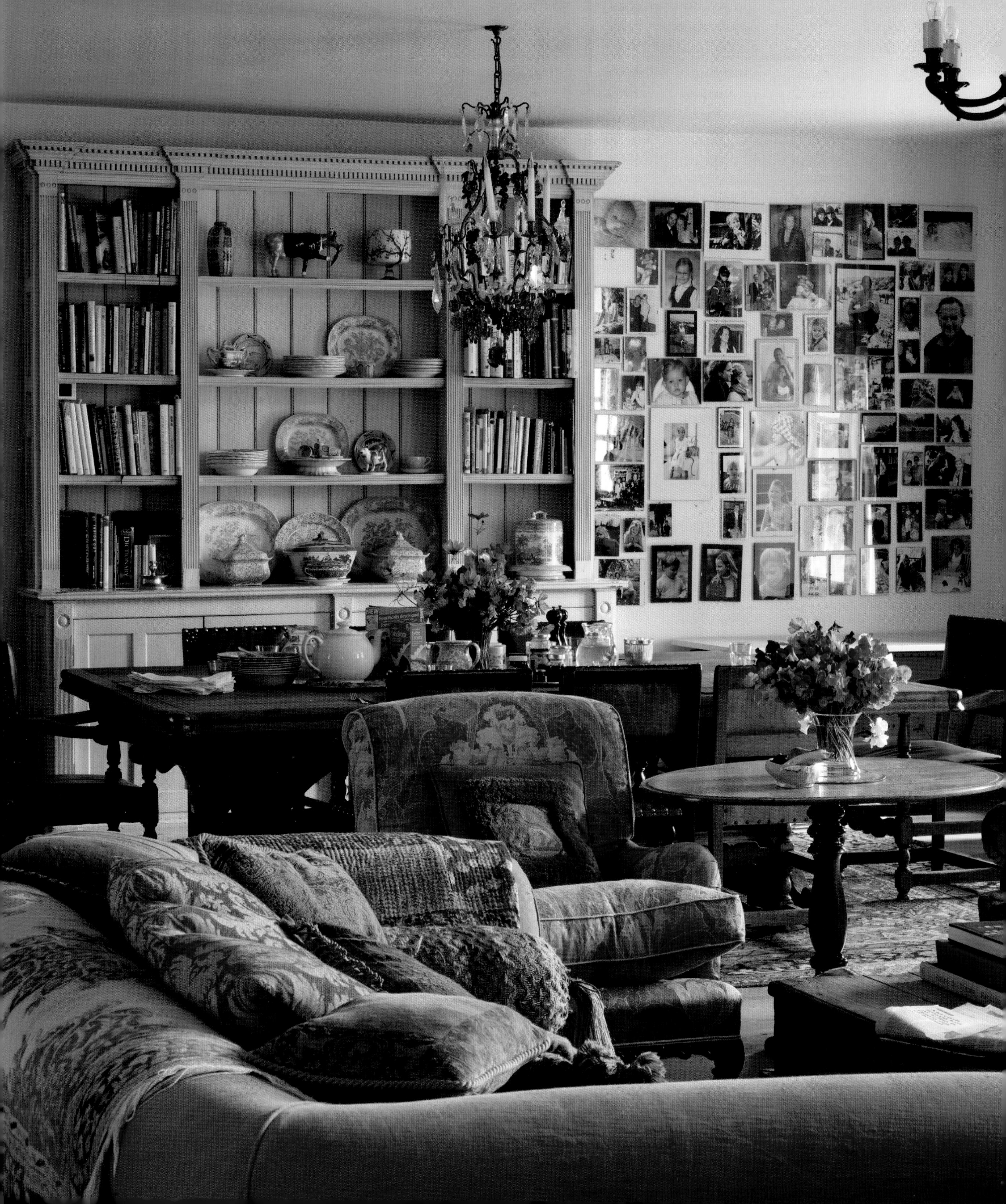

THIS PAGE: Lying on a flagged floor of Cotswold stone that came from five different sources are the family's two dogs, Labrador Buster and Bernie the Airedale.

OPPOSITE: The storage cabinet is originally French but bought in Bradford-on-Avon after John Robinson had successfully bet on a horse race.

Gradually the project expanded so that the Bannermans, invited to create not just a new indoor pool but also a 50-foot drawing room and a master bedroom complex, came up with the notion of designing this around the 'ruins' of a medieval monastery, complete with cloister supporting an orangery. 'They gave us a scale model they'd made, showing what we should build,' says John Robinson, 'and the result turned out exactly as they proposed.' In fact, the Robinsons not only loved the Bannerman scheme but went on to extend the work still further so as to include a walled vegetable garden, formal water feature, thatched boathouse, parkland planting and so forth.

Hence Euridge Manor came to assume its present fantastical form. Since an enormous amount of excavation had to be carried out on site, this provided much of the stone used in the building work, not least for the present indoor swimming pool and its surrounds as well as a cloister that runs along one side of the building. Meanwhile, the Bannermans' interest in architectural salvage meant they were able to incorporate several old gothic church windows into the finished structure, thereby making it at least partly authentic.

But Euridge is true to the spirit of the eighteenth-century Gothick movement in fearlessly combining a number of different styles. Whilst the 'ruins' are in the High Gothic

Euridge is true to the spirit of the eighteenth-century Gothick movement in fearlessly combining a number of different styles.

manner of the fifteenth century, the exterior of drawing room/bedroom extension, for example, is more Jacobean in spirit and in turn this part of the house's interiors owes something to early nineteenth-century design. Meanwhile, the terraced gardens and large formal pool are essentially Italianate high baroque in spirit, indebted in their character to the work in seventeenth-century Rome of Bernini and Borromini. At the far end of the pool is a fantastical thatched boathouse, as yet empty of boats but surely awaiting some ornate craft

The totality is a triumphant achievement and demonstrates eclecticism's potential.

with coloured sails that would not look out of place in a Tiepolo fresco. Inside the house, the furnishings are equally diverse and very often a single piece will have come from several sources. Typically in the family room section of the kitchen the stone chimneypiece is a composite, its sides made from a pair of gateposts, its top incorporating some new and some old material. Everywhere one turns it is impossible to pronounce with confidence on the origins of what can be seen. Nevertheless, the totality is a triumphant achievement and demonstrates eclecticism's potential. Gothic purists might not approve but Gothick romantics certainly will.

ABOVE: Directly above the drawing room is the main bedroom, dominated by a pilastered bedhead which, like so much else at Euridge, is of recent vintage despite appearances to the contrary. It faces a glazed gallery with views over the valley beyond the gardens.

OPPOSITE: Partly screened by galleries of columns, one end of the bedroom serves as the Robinsons' bathroom. The matching mirrors over the sinks have their frames silvered rather than gilded.

THIS PAGE AND OPPOSITE: The principal guest bedroom holds an old leather and mahogany bed acquired from Ralph Lauren. The screen of free-standing columns with their papyrus capitals, as well as the entablature above, came from an antique shop in Bradford-on-Avon. As with the master bedroom, all bathroom facilities are on the other side of this screen.

INDEX

ACKNOWLEDGMENTS

The author would like to express his sincere thanks to all those house owners whose properties feature in this book and whose kindness, tolerance and help during its preparation were very much appreciated. He would also like to express his gratitude to the many owners who allowed him to visit their homes even though, for various reasons, these do appear in the present work. For their generous advice and support, he thanks the following: Lucy Cavendish; Alicia Clements; Katie Dashwood; Ed and Erica Fairfax-Lucy; Jack and Susannah Hanbury-Tenison; Jane and Jeremy Harrison; the late Miranda Iveagh; Shawn Kholucy; Tim Knox; Bill and Daphne Montgomery; Harry Mount; Solveig and Humphrey Stone; Will and Sophy Topley; Sue Trevor.